So Much Love, So Little Money

So Much Love,
So Little Money

LYN IRVINE

FABER AND FABER

24 Russell Square

London

First published in mcmlvii
by Faber and Faber Limited
24 Russell Square London W.C.1
Second impression July mcmlvii
Printed in Great Britain by
Latimer Trend & Co Ltd Plymouth

Contents

Foreword

Without the conviction that this book would be anonymous, I could not have written it happily—which is the same as saying that I could not have written it at all. It reveals much that was tender and intimate in the lives of people who themselves shrank from the least trace of publicity, and although the revelation cannot hurt now, the screen of anonymity seemed to me important. However my publishers assure me that it no longer acts as a screen, and I have submitted to their advice.

As it is not a work of scholarship, I might dispense with acknowledgements, but I want to thank all the friends who believed that some day I should finish another book. One I must name for her special kindness and encouragement—Antoinette Esher. And it was her final comment when she read the MS.—'So much love and so little money!'—that gave me the title for which I was looking.

LYN IRVINE

August 1956

9

CHAPTER ONE

Starting from Berwick-on-Tweed

It was in March of 1892 that my father married and brought his wife from her remote and beautiful home in County Limerick to a tight little brick house near the church where he was minister—Princes Road Presbyterian Church in Liverpool. An entry in his diary four months after the wedding, written in my mother's hand, runs: 'Very depressed (& faithless) as to domestic prospects in general.' My mother had practically no money of her own and my father's stipend was £350 a year, and both were handicapped by the style in which they had been brought up, not lavish indeed, but with plenty of domestic help. In November 1892 the diary comes to an end and it was nine years before my father kept one again, which indicates that there proved to be good cause for his depression as he looked forward in the fifth month of his marriage. But from 1st January 1901 until 25th June 1949, the day before he died, he never failed to make an entry or note the quarter from which the wind blew.

In the nine years of no record my three brothers and my elder sister were born, all in Liverpool. In 1899 my father accepted a call to Wallace Green Church, Berwick-on-Tweed, and under Friday, 3rd May 1901 he wrote in the recently resumed diary: 'Beautiful day in morn. Reached home 5 a.m. Baby born 8.15 a.m.' He had been in London for the church synod, but left hurriedly for home at 8.45 p.m. on the Thursday evening, and after a long slow journey saw the sun rising over the sea as he approached Berwick. On May 4th the midwife arrived, but I had beaten her by thirty-six hours, a miscalculation not so serious with a fifth child as a first or second. My father's unmarried sister Christina was there to help, and my mother after a late start was beginning to know a thing or two about children. In her early twenties her ignorance had been great, and while she was engaged to my father she went to stay with friends in the north of Ireland in order to study the management of small children. She began by bringing the little things to breakfast carefully buttoned into clean nightgowns put on back to front.

At Fort Etna—the name of my mother's home—the girls had been taught by a succession of home-sick English governesses. Much time was spent practising the piano, usually before breakfast in a very cold schoolroom, and a great deal went more happily picking flowers in the fields and ditches and tying them into little posies to comfort the poor people in Limerick Hospital. They grew up tender-hearted, pious, knowing nothing of the world. 'You will never set the Thames on fire,' said one disheartened governess, and pricked by the criticism, as she grew older my mother sat up late into the night endeavouring to improve her mind, and brewing black coffee to keep herself awake. She read *Trilby* when it came out, and then blushed to admit it in a polite London drawing-room. By virtue of her great vitality and many natural gifts, she survived the first ten desperate years of married life without losing her courage or her looks. I remember her in 1904 coming up the garden path after morning church. I ran to welcome her and she bent from her great height, bowing the long grey ostrich feather in her hat and giving me her cheek to kiss through her veil. It was as cool as a bunch of snowdrops.

We lived at Berwick-on-Tweed until 1908 and the setting of the town and its surroundings puts a seal on all my under-seven memories. Wallace Green Manse, 3 Wellington Terrace, stood on the ancient wall of the town looking south across the Tweed, and nothing obscured the view eastward to the open sea, for it was the last house in the terrace. Westward, up the river beyond the quay, there was the old town bridge and the tall, elegant Royal Border Bridge beyond it. The unfriendly concrete arches of the Royal Tweed Bridge had not then been conceived. In stormy weather the waves breaking against the walls under our house shot up into the air above the battlements and broke in spray over the green mounds between the portholes. Little heavy cannon pointed their muzzles through these portholes and we used to try the strength of our spindly arms on the cannon balls lying ready beside them. In those days the walls were still under the care of the War Office, which closed them for one day every year, and set a sentry in a red coat on guard near our house with rifle and bayonet fixed. The boys baited him, dashing past him on to the forbidden ground. It was very like a game that we played among ourselves, called Tom Tiddler's Ground, on the same walls on less important days.

We had no garden in front of the Manse, only an area with iron railings, the pavement, the gravel drive of the

walls and then the battlements. Behind, heavily over-
shadowed by our own house and our neighbour's, lay a
narrow strip of walled garden and over the wall at the
bottom stood the British School, from which the sound
of children endlessly chanting the alphabet and their two-
times wove itself into my thoughts and games. On the
left of the path to the back gate lay a little strip of earth
divided by glazed brown earthenware imitations of rope
into five small plots. Most of these were given up to
games and experiments unfriendly to any kind of growth.
But my brother Jack persevered and grew a thick crop of
very tall plants and in this forest he placed a very small
stool, and there he sat, almost hidden from view, much
to our envy and admiration. A malting-house lay beyond
the school, pouring out its rich sweet smell to battle with
the clean astringent sea-smells. My mother bought great
brown jars of malt to fatten us, and sometimes the
malting-house cats came to visit us, wild and scrawny
beasts, like the cats in Bewick's woodcuts. Once a nearly
empty jar of malt was drained into a saucer and then the
saucer left over night on the kitchen dresser. Next day a
little mouse was found drowned dead in the malt in the
saucer, and the cook, puzzled how to deal with this, laid
the saucer in front of a visiting cat, which forthwith
seized the mouse and ran round and round the kitchen
wearing the saucer of malt on its nose.

This kitchen and the other rooms level with the garden
at the back and the area at the front were all dark and
damp, and the bedroom of this faithful cook, our only
maidservant, Mary, seemed little better than the lair of a
wild animal. But the appearance of Wellington Terrace
from the river and the walls pleased the eye. It was built
of freestone, with pillared porticoes and large regular

sash windows. Harpoons carved in the panels of the door of Number One were the fancy of its first owner, a master in the Berwick whaling fleet in the first part of the nineteenth century. After the cramped and dismal house in Liverpool the spaciousness of the Berwick manse and its unique position delighted my parents. In cold weather the height of the rooms and the vast amount of unheated space in halls and passages and stairways prevented the temperature inside from rising much higher than that outside, but fifty years ago people wore very thick clothes. Skirts were ankle-length and lined, petticoats of flannel, and everyone wore woollen stockings in winter. If we felt cold in bed we used to rub our feet up and down between the sheets until they shone, which seemed to give an impression of warmth.

My mother's bedroom was above the dining-room and looked south over the Tweed. It was in this room that she hung on to the bars at the head of her bed in child-labour, crying to herself 'Oh what a fool I have been', until Dr. Maclagan (son and father too of famous Berwick doctors, and himself greatly loved) tossed her a big handkerchief soaked in chloroform, in which she buried her face, and presently awoke to the sight of another baby, and with it the banishment of all self-reproach. Across the landing from this bedroom was my father's study with its window south and another window looking east to the sea, the best study he ever had and the room he enjoyed most in his life.

Berwick was in those days very unconscious of its own charm—a miniature town in lovely surroundings, sown from ancient seed. It must still be unconscious of the beauty of its stonework, for in 1954 masons were coating the pier with concrete. I mourn the disappearance of the huge blocks of stone of which it was built a hundred and fifty years ago, each stone different and worthy to be a monument, each having answered back in its own way through the years to sea and sun and rain and frost, to the footsteps of fishermen and the hands and knees of children. Each stone with a little care good for another hundred years. Along this once lovely pier, finished off with its bold little lighthouse, my father took his walk every morning, however rough the weather might be, unless the breakers overflowed the causeway. At no time in his long life was he happier than during the nine years at Berwick and the serene and youthful face in his farewell photograph bears witness to this. A routine which continued for nearly forty years became set in Berwick and was little altered when he moved to Aberdeen. He rose early without an alarm clock, and gathered his family for reading and prayer before breakfast was served at eight. After breakfast he took his constitutional and then went to his study to prepare his sermons and addresses until dinner-time at one o'clock. Then came the pastoral visiting, the session meetings, presbytery meetings, mothers' meetings, and later in the day the weekly prayer meeting or the men's discussion group or a social gathering. We heard all these activities announced on Sunday at church and considered them as natural and necessary as the phases of the moon. Saturday was spent in retreat, conning and memorizing his two sermons, but he came out of retreat to bury the dead in the afternoon, and sometimes to take a country walk with one or two of his family.

I never accompanied my father on a pastoral visit and I am not quite sure what he did. With the sick or the bereaved he must have read the Bible and prayed, but with the others there was surely some general conversation, for morsels were carried home to us, like the little bits of wedding cake that my mother used to bring back from weddings in her handkerchief. The father of one old parishioner had fought in the Battle of Waterloo, but never saw a Frenchy on the field. 'And what d'ye think of Lloyd George?' asked an old woman in Aberdeen. 'Och mon, yon's aebody's doggie for a bane.'

This happy period at Berwick coloured far more than the first seven years of my life. Although the fifth child I was the first that my father had much leisure to enjoy. I was perky, imitative, ambitious and curious. In answer to my questions he took an apple in one hand and an orange in the other and explained the Solar System. He taught me to read. Then he provided me with a tiny golf club, a cleek, and showed me the correct stance and hold, and how to hit the heads off daisies. I was much too small for any club one could buy ready-made, so he had a specially short shaft put into the smallest head available. He sang 'Oh dear what can the matter be?' to cheer me up when I was sad, and piloted me through many plates of tapioca pudding by reciting *The Tale of Peter Rabbit*. When I was six he bought me the pocket edition of *Alice in Wonderland*, inscribing it delicately on the fly-leaf, and my brothers complained that I was spoilt because I so often wheedled a penny out of him to buy a Dutch doll at Janet Walker's toy shop. In such ways the sails were trimmed and the rudder set for a long voyage.

The primer which my father bought for me had very glossy paper and the picture which headed each lesson was as bright as stained glass when the sun shines through it. This made it very pleasant to learn to read, and the following year, when I was six, I went to Miss Fisher's

School where I wove strips of silver paper in and out of bands of pink paper. I also arranged leaves on a card and waited for a big girl to come with a wire grid and a toothbrush dipped in indian ink. Rubbing the toothbrush over the grid she skilfully sprayed the card. When the fine shading of ink dried, I lifted the leaves off and threw them away and admired the result of all this ingenuity, and glued a little calendar to the bottom of the card. The little girl who sat behind me pulled my hair until I complained to the Miss Fisher in charge, and then to my horror I found that I had done the wrong thing. Either I ought to have borne it in silence or found somebody else to do the complaining for me. The face of the little girl who pulled, and the little boy who was her ally, are the first contemporary faces that I remember clearly. They stand out like little stone carvings, whimseys of the mason, on an otherwise smooth, blank wall—half-shut, hurt eyes of the little girl and the angry accusing face of the little boy.

The first spoken words that I could swear to having heard date from the same time. One morning going to school with my father, who had given up his cherished walk along the pier in order to conduct me, I began to brag. Possibly the older girls at school had been petting me as a newcomer and stimulating the vanity so carefully checked at home. My father let me run on a few minutes and then gently broke in: 'Suppose we talk a little less about ourselves.' Those were his words, not one different, not one more or less. After a moment given up to scorching comprehension, I dashed off and ran far ahead on the road to school, unable to face out my shame at his side. It was a snub which hurt without achieving its purpose, as this book testifies.

It was on the way to Miss Fisher's, at the top of Bank-hill, that the wind once caught my petticoats and blew me up into the air. I came down on the grass, not hurt but very much frightened. This experience made the story and pictures of Flying Robert in the end of Struwwelpeter seem very plausible. After Flying Robert my favourite page was the picture at the beginning, of the Christmas tree and the presents. I first saw the light that never was on land or sea burn in those candles. I wanted it to be real and yet I did not want it to be real, for fear that the reality would never be so beautiful and exciting.

At this stage only a few scenes equalled pictures in importance. I remember a little white cottage on a cliff, hot and bright in the sun, with a green parrot in a wicker cage hanging from a hook by the open door. And I see the sky, as it might be for the first time. A dark cloud lay like a saucepan lid over the world that I knew—the bridges, the harbour, the fishing boats, and the tower on the corner of the walls where the black storm cone was raised on a rope to warn the fishermen. As we passed the tower and our house came in sight the dark lid in the sky split from end to end with a wonderful tearing light and the thunder came tumbling to the earth. Elsa, my big sister, covered my eyes with one hand, the eyes so newly able to see, and hurried me home in the go-cart.

I have another memory of Elsa and the go-cart. Someone had given her a silver Canadian half-dollar piece and she wished to change it into English money in order to buy a packet of Dolly Headache Cure for my mother, troubled at that time with headaches such as are fairly common among mothers with six children under twelve. So pushing me and taking my youngest brother Edward to help, Elsa went the round of the banks in Berwick, sometimes asking herself and sometimes sending in Edward, hoping that his sailor suit and angel face might make the right impression. We were very poor indeed, yet there was always Mary cooking and cleaning and making fires, and at one stage we had a nurse too, who wore a black silk bonnet with ribbons under her chin. She had a horrid flat way of saying: 'You needn't call for your mother, she's not coming up.' The experience of not being able to reach my mother because of the barrier of this nurse Maggie first set in my heart the terror of death taking her beyond all call, and from that time until I grew up I trembled for her life, without which my own seemed insupportable. If I had dared to believe that she would live to be a great-grandmother, as she did with the greatest ease, the whole tenor of my childhood would have been altered.

I remember when I was three visiting the nursery at 1 Wellington Terrace where Captain Allenby lived. His son Jaffy and my younger sister Yda[1] were both infants and lay being changed on their respective nurses' knees. I stood gazing at them and pitying them for not knowing how to complain about their heads hanging down before a blazing fire, when Maggie told me sharply to go away because it was very rude to look. The twentieth century has had its minor triumphs and the extinction of such Maggies may be counted among them.

[1] Her godmother, Yda Thompson, had been herself called after a Dutch friend who spelt the name so, and it unfortunately never occurred to our parents that my sister might later on be suspected of altering her name from Ida to Yda in order to attract attention. They seem to have had an affection for the letter Y, for when I shortened in babyhood the name which had been handed down to me from my mother, they replaced the I by Y in that too.

Whenever I lost my temper with this younger sister in later days it was the custom to remind me of my delight when she was born, but constant reminding by others merely dulls the original imprint, and I remember nothing of that last week in August 1904 except catching my hair in a fly-paper in my mother's bedroom. It was a quarto sheet with a border of small newsprint or advertisements, and I had the distinction of having my hair washed in turpentine to remove the stickiness and the dead flies. The previous winter when I was two, I had developed a long unexplained illness. My mother believed that I caught cold one day that she pushed me out in the go-cart without a rug round my legs, when the wind proved much colder than she expected. I swelled up and was feverish for many weeks, and I have a pin-hole memory of this time, of waking out of nightmare in my father's arms, and seeing to my surprise that we were in the kitchen, with a lamp burning on the table and my mother and someone else standing by. This early illness made me feel weary for some time and when the baby Yda began to be pushed out in the perambulator and I to toddle alongside, the advantages of being a baby seemed great to me. I climbed or was lifted to peer over the edge of the pram. I saw the little half-moon down pillow with its frilly edge and thought it must be nice when people didn't expect you to do anything but lay your head there and look at the sky and the trees.

When a child fell ill we had an oil lamp with a huge red shade of dimpled and purfled glass which stood on the bedroom floor, cheerful and friendly, but giving out little heat. A coal fire was much better, and that we called having 'Arrabella on the Ceiling' in reference to some forgotten story about the shadows thrown up by the firelight, shadows which in those days included at least one or perhaps two jointed gas brackets near the mantelpiece, limbs of the dear dancing goddess of sick children, Arrabella. Children to-day are more lucid and prosaic than we were. One game of enduring charm consisted merely in hiding behind the heavy rep curtains of the dining-room window and popping one's face through the slit to cry 'Gossamer Sails', making as one did so a new kind of face to surprise the watchers, something funny or terrifying thought up in the dark space between the curtains and the window itself. On our ambling walks there was nothing to suggest a mechanized age except the telegraph wires, and those I understood as little as any Patagonian or Eskimo. I scrambled into the hedgerow to lay my ear against the rough warm cheek of the telegraph pole and hear the Queen's kettle boiling.

At Berwick our usual playground was the shore and our favourite walk, like my father's, the pier. Its wall was stepped to provide a narrow footpath to the lighthouse when a very high tide and a stormy sea made the causeway itself impassable. This path was a famous test of sureness of foot. About half-way out to sea the pier bent away from the river mouth and reached out northwards. Just before the bend, Crabwater Batt stretched down into the water, a great ramp of rounded stones, slippery with green seaweed. Here the salmon-fishers were often busy, and we stopped to watch them row out in their cobles, dropping the nets from the stern as they went and fetching in a sweet curve back to the pier again. On our way home we passed the nets not in use, furbled with scraps of seaweed, spread out to dry on walls and stretches of shingle that lay above the water-line. We picked up broken and lost floats, and if we found seaweed juicy and in good condition we broke off some berries and sucked them, until the day when a playfellow told us that an earwig came out of her berry. Near the drying nets and the tall old houses, where the kitchens were full of herrings turning into kippers, stood a small house made of an upturned coble raised on low wooden walls, the whole tarred and pitched and much blistered by the sun, but a very agreeable shape and size. Dr. Lethbridge in his book *Merlin's Island* suggests that both the name—from a word meaning originally a skin boat—and the shape of the coble must have come with Aidan and his twelve monks from Iona when they built the first church on Lindisfarne in the first half of the seventh century.

Lindisfarne we called Holy Island, and all went on an expedition to see it when I was very small indeed. For a large young family it was quite a serious pilgrimage. We took the train to Beal and crossed the sands at low tide in a pony cart, the wide wet shining sands. With the preoccupation of a creature new to walking I noticed and never forgot the broad shallow steps, cobbled and paved, leading to the south entrance of the castle, but everything else faded. When my father first went to Berwick the castle was derelict, but in 1903 Mr. Edward Hudson persuaded Lutyens to restore it and turn it into a country house, and so the fine work was begun which took nine years to complete. To Goswick, a little nearer than Beal, we also made excursions and picnicked on the shore, for my father used to golf there. Every spring we went to Janet Walker's to buy new pails for the beach, and these were simple, solid and beautiful, snowy-white inside and green or red or blue outside with a few gold stripes. The smell of fresh enamel was strong and delicious. Janet Walker sold many lovely things, glass marbles and snowstorms and dolls' feeding bottles with very long tubes of rubber joining the teat to the bottle, resembling a type of baby's bottle already out of date. After the three eldest went to live with our grandfather and go to school in Birkenhead, I used to feed my dolls with such bottles, playing all alone in a very quiet house. The quietness felt light and soft, yet substantial, like a down quilt, and I loved it. My darkey doll, called Dinah, was my favourite, partly because her heathen origin and need for conversion made it correct for me to play with her on Sunday, a pleasant idea of my mother's. It was largely because I needed a new doll that my mother took me with her to Edinburgh for the day in the spring of 1905 or 1906. For this outing I had a new white flannel skirt, pleated, and a white jersey. Perhaps I ought to have had a coat too but I think that my mother could afford no more and did not like to put an old coat over my pretty jersey and skirt. Old Uncle Scott, my great-uncle, whom we visited in the Manse at Musselburgh, fixed me at once with his stern eyes and said: 'Lilian, that child is not sufficiently clad.' But it was a fine clear day and when I leaned back to look up at the high buildings in Princes Street they seemed to be wheeling grandly away over the blue sky. We went down area steps to the basket shop and bought a miniature basket with lids on either side of the handle. Then came the climax, the search for the doll, and it may have been Jenners which had a big room underground given up to dolls, all with faces perhaps monotonously good-tempered, but not one of them vulgar or false or silly like the dolls made to-day. One doll, perched in a place of honour in the middle of a glass case, wore a gold chain and a ruby pendant over flounced rose-coloured silk. She was perfection. But even as I gazed at her my mother was discussing with the attendant the price of a naked doll with a very durable body covered with white kid, firmly stitched and ingeniously jointed. The kid was slightly soiled, otherwise she would have been far too expensive. I am sure that she looked well when my mother had dressed her, but I never liked the new doll. Papier-maché bodies with china heads were then common, and a very precious Irish doll called Lucy melted before our eyes when we gave her a cold bath in the basin. Her pretty head on the wire prongs which guided her eyes was laid away in cotton wool for thirty years. Then my mother, preparing for a grandchild, sent it with a golden tress of real hair from a family shearing to the Dolls' Hospital in Chelsea. She returned with a new body and hair hanging to her waist and promises in her new state to wear out packs and sets of great ones.

At a church sale in Berwick someone gave me a doll's cot made out of two halves of an eggshell, complete with doll, pillow, sheets, blanket and a padded quilt. The Cairns came from Ayton to visit us, and I showed it to Alison, then two or so, with a warning to be very careful. But she did not understand and crushed it instantly in her little paw as she sat on the dining-room sofa with her short legs in black boots sticking straight out. It was a horsehair sofa and the broken hairs always pricked one badly behind the knees. Mrs. Cairns plied Alison with a huge glass of milk which looked overwhelmingly rich to me.

All through my childhood we picnicked incessantly. It was not much to my father's taste; he preferred a good walk or a bicycle ride and a meal at home in comfort afterwards. But my mother loved impromptu meals in the fresh air. She was as clever as a gipsy with twigs and leaves, but when the wind was strong or fuel wet and scarce, it sometimes took a long time for the kettle to boil —and the water must never be poured on the tea-leaves until it had reached a rolling boil. We grew indifferent to rain and would bathe while the drops pimpled the smooth water, and then sit round the fire with our coats over our heads. We always tried to get away from other people, excepting fishermen, coastguards, ploughmen and shepherds, whom we accepted as part of the land-scape or seascape. As many of our holidays were spent in the Scottish Highlands, rain, flies and midges enter into many memories. One moorland fly made a dead set at my mother and scrambled inside the glass of her pince-nez over and over again. My mother, always more Irish when in trouble, felt sure that he mistook it for a window-pane.

From Berwick we made an expedition every spring to Marshall Meadows to pick the snowdrops which grew so thickly under the trees in the wood at the back of the garden. Beyond this wood ran the railway line to Edin-burgh, and beyond that a meadow and over the meadow lay the sea, at the bottom of great red cliffs full of sea birds. There was only one way down to the little rocky bay, through a smuggler's tunnel carved in the rock. I found it again nearly fifty years later, long and dark and eerie just as I remembered it, and went down the slippery passage to the bright water and the crying birds at the far end, a place undisturbed by man, and yet without peace. I preferred the seagulls that came to Berwick in their twos and threes, and the solitary wail followed by a quick dying cadence so often to be heard in the stillness at low tide. It is a sound entirely without beauty and yet refreshing to the ears, and the emotions that it stirred, while all my own, seemed to have their roots elsewhere. So I felt and still feel listening to the plaintive but far sweeter call of the peewit, and I think that my father would have understood me. He had returned home when we came to the Borders. His grandparents were buried in Jedburgh Abbey graveyard and five earlier generations in Staplegordon, in the hills above Langholm. Of covenanting stock, these ancestors were at first crofters, coopers and farmers, but after 1800 their descendants turned to the Church and to business, moving south, as my grandfather did in the fifties, to become a pioneer in West African trade before he settled down to the life of a Liverpool city man.

I dreamt of both heaven and hell while still living at Berwick. In my dream heaven was a gay place. One played—I see the interweaving groups of happy children —and felt delightful. Hell also appeared as a place for play, and again there were the little dancing figures, but I became aware that they danced with a hot and furtive glee, and that was all. I remembered my dream again when I read Lowell's comment upon an essay by Leslie Stephen on Jonathan Edwards the Calvinist: 'If he had only conceived of damnation as a spiritual state, the very horror of which consists (to our deeper apprehension) in its being delightful to who is in it, I could go along with him altogether.'[1] At five I would have gone along with Lowell. The comprehension of small children is always out of all proportion to their experience. In the cradle they can already distinguish between anger and mere irritation, between bravado and self-assurance, just as easily as the broad and simple differences of love and no-love, knowledge and ignorance. It is not surprising when

[1] I quote from Noël Annan's *Life of James Stephen*.

a child absorbs many subtle moral notions in a home where much sincere thought is given to such things, and although there may be good reasons for not teaching theology to young children, their incapacity to grasp it cannot be one of them. Ideas in fact are often easier to get straight than people. We had a *Story of the Bible*, a large old-fashioned selection of all the narrative parts of the Old and New Testaments, with black and white illustrations. The first chapter began with a picture of a bald-headed scribe with a quill pen whom I took to be God writing down the story of the creation. When I first went to church in Berwick I was interested but not very surprised to find that God appeared in person in a sober black suit, carrying up a copy of the book he had written so long ago and laying it on the desk in the pulpit. Then he went back to the vestry and fetched my father to read it for us. The picture in *The Story of the Bible* was so close a likeness of our beadle, there was at first no doubt in my mind, but after a time I altered my idea a little and took him as not exactly and in all his activities God, but a divinely authorized understudy. I apprehended dedication and some suffering in my father on a Sunday, for he was an extremely nervous and conscientious man, and the pulpit seemed to be his cross, to which he was led by our Wallace Green God. When we left Berwick all this fell to pieces as the church officer at the South United Free Church in Aberdeen did not resemble the picture of God in the least. Yet for a long time I felt that the figure mounting the pulpit stairs in his long silk robe went to a mystical punishment for the sins of the congregation.

The Bible influenced our attitude to dreams, for it was full of stories of interesting and important dreamers, and the older I grew the more I regarded dreams as intended

for the enrichment and guidance of life. Without them
sleep would lose much of its refreshment and charm, and
waking life become like water without reflections on its
surface. When, very much later, it became indiscreet to
tell one's dreams to anyone but a psychiatrist, I wrote
them in a book for my own entertainment. Every age
needs to find something improper; in my babyhood petticoats were as improper as dreams are now. A young
woman out for a walk with her young man in Berwick
had the dreadful experience of losing her petticoat. She
was passing my mother—who was wheeling me in the
perambulator—as she felt the tape give way. She skipped
over the garment as it fell and stuffed it rapidly into the
pram whispering her name and address to my mother
and continuing her walk with an aplomb ever after held
up for our admiration.

Early in 1908 a church in Croydon called my father, at
the same time as the church in Aberdeen did. He chose
Aberdeen for the sake of the education of his children.
But he was well known and already much valued in the
English Presbyterian Church, while in the United Free
Church of Scotland he was a newcomer, with the great
disadvantage of an English accent, and by the time that
his great integrity won him recognition in Scotland, he
was past his middle years. But he saw very well what he
was doing and made his choice for the sake of his children. The three older ones, away from home during the
term, could be moved to schools at Aberdeen, which
delighted them all. My mother's indulgent rule was
much preferred to that of Aunt Christina. As for Edward,
Yda and myself, we were still at an age when the new is
taken for granted as better, and before the call was confirmed, Edward wrote 'Ask and ye shall receive' on a

29

piece of paper and pinned it above his bed to keep his courage up. Yda, aged three and less doubting, chanted 'Aberdeen haddies, Aberdeen haddies' from her pram as my embarrassed mother pushed her up the High Street. But it was all right, the call came and was accepted, and Edward, now ten and my mother's right hand, painted all the bedroom chairs in gay colours to match the pretty wallpapers chosen for the Aberdeen manse. The paint upset him and he fainted in church as my father pronounced the benediction at our very last morning service in Wallace Green. My father noticed his pale face and swooped down the pulpit stairs so fast that the sleeves of his gown floated up like huge black wings. He caught Edward just as he slumped forward on to the book rest, and carried him into the vestry.

If I think of my parents just as parents, I see my father as an eagle hovering above us, and although he seemed quite far and detached his keen blue eye never left us. But my mother was a tigress among her cubs, ready to defend us to the death. Aunt Christina annoyed her by saying: 'Lilian will never be content until she has a dozen children,' but it is a pity that she had only six. She could have borne and reared twice as many and cared for each as individually and intensely, for hearts like hers and my father's enlarge easily to meet all claims. We felt them both too fussy and anxious, guarding us often from dangers which seemed hypothetical. But my mother's extreme watchfulness over food, for example, was partly responsible for our escaping serious illnesses. When she suspected the purity of a milk supply, she sent a specimen to the city analyst, who rather more than confirmed her suspicions, and then she boiled our milk and changed to another dairy. I think that she was incapable of having a favourite among us, or perhaps it is truer to say that she usually had a favourite, the child that she loved most being the one least in luck at that moment. If she felt one of us to be in a rut, she called a family conclave and put the problem before all the others, and then there would be a truce to teasing, or a treat or a gift provided. So at one stage, when I seemed low, it was decided that I needed a pet, and a Hartz Mountain Roller, a most voluble canary, was found to cheer me up. But if there was one among us that suited my mother better than another, it was Edward, who was called after her own father. She had a stabbing memory of nearly losing him as a very small child. He slipped from her in one of the narrow old streets of Berwick, and when she missed him and began to look frantically round, he reappeared on all fours from beneath the wheels of a moving dray. Owing to his being very young and yet not young enough to be watched over like his two baby sisters, Edward got into more difficulties than the rest of the family. He was lost again on a family picnic up the Tweed in the wood called the Plantation. Soon Archie the eldest brother hunted him down, but the experience had unnerved Edward who was heard saying at family prayers: 'Lead us not into the Plantation but deliver us from Evil.' A cousin of my father's once carried him up his supper in bed, and never forgot the small boy sitting there solemnly and asking her as soon as she appeared why the lightning fell to the earth.

We went very early to bed, and like children at all times, we never slept as much as the grown-ups wished and expected, and the idea that we ought to be asleep always shook its finger at us. So it required courage to complain of lying awake, to ask for food or drink, not because anyone would be angry, but because we were convinced of its irregularity. Eventually I became obsessed by the fear of hunger as I lay awake long after everyone else was in bed, and I used to creep down after midnight in the total dark and silence of the house to find a biscuit, the operation taking a very long time because of my care not to wake anyone. But just as a very small child learning to walk may be given confidence by seeing an adult trip and fall, so I was helped in this trouble by seeing Great-aunt Agnes cut four inches off a French loaf as evening approached, and carry it openly to her bedroom to eat in the night. After that I used my little wooden treasure-box with a lock and key to hide some pieces of bread. They soon became too stale and hard to eat, but as I never wanted to eat them that was of no consequence.

We felt an important distinction between misery before going to sleep and misery after having slept for a time. That, though rarer, shocked no one. If a child woke with a nightmare, my father—a much lighter sleeper than my mother—hurried to soothe and spoke so kindly that courage was soon restored; and no objection was ever raised to the request for a night-light, a little squat candle which burnt very softly and slowly in a saucer of water. I was pleased to find recently in an old letter from my grandmother to my grandfather a request for saucers for night-lights to be brought down to a holiday house in Llandudno. 'Please bring Opera Glass, 2 common white saucers for night lights, a church service. Don't bring your nail brush, I have bought one here. . . .'

My parents did in a way exchange roles at night. My mother fell into such a deep sleep as soon as her head touched the pillow that she was scarcely capable of waking before six in the morning, or scarcely herself if she did struggle up, and we might have been sadly placed sometimes but for the alertness and patience of my father. By day he had his pastoral duties and drew away a little from the details of the home. We grew shy of him by day, and he of us. It was his part then to check my mother in her readiness to embrace financial ruin for our happiness, his part also to greet our more outlandish guests (who fascinated her) with that touch of reserve which discouraged them from living with us indefinitely, and in general to head off her impulse with his caution. In all this he was harder on himself than on her. But I do not think that he was burdened with many theories about bringing up children, and my mother certainly had none. As in cooking, recipes were useless for one never had the ingredients necessary, the only thing to do was to guess and taste and pray. She remembered the troubles of her own childhood and her rule of thumb was to avoid a repetition of them in ours. So we must never be criticized unkindly or made to blush, or be frightened of the dark, or wear shoes that pinched. But the great pleasures of her childhood, singing Moody and Sankey hymns and picking wild flowers, she hoped would be our pleasures too. Rather ahead of her generation, she believed in sunshine, and even tried to cure me of influenza (which she had diagnosed as the Doldrums) by walking me up and down outside the house on her arm one bright cold morning. Her remorse was great when the doctor excluded the Doldrums.

When the moment came to get into the four-wheeler and drive away for ever from the Berwick manse, that beautiful place where I had been born and lived so happily for nearly seven years, I felt so excited and pleased that I

c   33

was astonished to observe a fearful change come over the face of our good Mary as she stood on the pavement when the door of the cab was closed. It seemed to disintegrate, twist and crumple up. She tried to see us all for the last time through her tears, then she threw her apron right over her head and turned away. I cannot remember her normal face at all, only that hideous mask which puzzled me greatly until my mother said something to connect it with grief. Her dreaminess had long been legendary. Pots of tea often rattled up in the service lift to the pantry, filled with boiling water only. Soon after this she married a Northumberland fisherman and went to live in Boulmer. She called one of her children after me and when I lived in London many years later she was still in touch with us, 'Berwick Mary', and used to post me enormous boxes of snowdrops in the spring.

CHAPTER TWO

The Scottish Grandfather

As long as we lived in Berwick it was our custom every Christmas to go to Birkenhead and stay with our grandparents at 18 Devonshire Road. Just as no one regards 10 Downing Street as a postal address, so we never saw or heard the word eighteen as merely the number of a house, or Devonshire Road as the name of a quiet respectable street, but rather felt those three words together to be a residential title full of meaning. It would have surprised me to know that very few people upon hearing it smelt at once the aroma of the kedgeree served there for Sunday breakfast or felt that they were directing their thoughts to the headquarters of well-ordered and tranquil living. It was only a tall, dull house with a tiny garden and a dark uninviting bath which had wooden doors like a box bed in a Scottish farmhouse. But my grandfather had lived at 18 Devonshire Road since the sixties and it was furnished with many exotic treasures which he had brought back from the Gold Coast some years before—ivory carvings, spears and swords, a native canoe, stools on which African chiefs had sat, and—best of all—a stuffed crocodile. From the

35

landing window by the pantry at the back of the house one had the pleasure of seeing a bright yellow garden through one pane of glass and a deep blue garden through another. I felt happy as I looked through the yellow pane and sunk in gloom as I looked through the blue, and I switched from one to the other enchanted by the rapid oscillation of my moods.

The journeys there and back in winter must have been a dread to both my parents, for we were all bad travellers. Being a cross-country journey, it took many hours in carriages sometimes heated with metal footwarmers filled with charcoal. My mother rolled us up in six rugs and laid us out on the seats, two a side. Once at Newcastle we were all disturbed by a woman who rushed in and tugged the rugs off our faces, looking for a lost child. Either she thought no woman could keep check of so large a flock, or she suspected my mother of being a professional baby-snatcher, returning home with a good haul. Her panic impressed me and I longed for many years to know if she ever found her lost child.

At 18 Devonshire Road the Christmas tree reached to the ceiling in the drawing-room and was piled around with presents. We joined all our numerous aunts and great-aunts, uncles and cousins, gathered at Grandpapa's bidding, and stood by the tree on Christmas Eve, singing 'Hark the Herod Angels Sing'—a very confusing carol about heavenly fifth-columnists. My grandfather had married twice. Five children, of whom my father was the eldest, survived of the first marriage, and two of the second. Five were sons and these all married, providing eventually more than twenty grandchildren, so that all family gatherings tended to be impressive. In summer we often met too, among the Border hills, or in the

north of Scotland, and picnics organized by my grandfather had a style of their own. We travelled to the site
in brakes, although some very active might bicycle, and
for the sake of the horses we often made a farm our ob-
jective. When we got there my grandfather would ask
for a table to be carried out into a field, or just into the
farmyard, so that he could eat his sandwiches in the
comfort that he liked and the style most suitable to him.
Before we began to eat we all stood to sing the Old
Hundredth.

> All people that on earth do dwell
> Sing to the Lord with cheerful voice.
> Him serve with mirth, His praise forth tell,
> Come ye before Him and rejoice.

The farmer's wife stood by, her hands folded on her
white apron, watching with gentle astonishment.

I remember my grandfather very well. I can conjure
up his appearance and his voice and his manner, and
more than that, when I think of him a sense of his per-
sonality pervades my mind, something whole and distinct and organic, which I cannot build up from his physical characteristics, or break down and analyse. This
sense of a person never seems to leave one, but is as per-
manent as an acquired skill such as walking or swimming
or riding a bicycle. Through it the people one has known
appear in dreams long after they are dead, bringing the
feeling of themselves back with wonderful potency. But
to talk of him in ordinary terms, he was rather a small
man, not stout, and always careful or even elegant in his
dress and equipment. He wore his tie drawn through a
gold ring of ancient pattern and he carried a malacca
cane, or in wet weather a smart umbrella with an ivory

handle. With the respect for the sun of a man who had lived in the tropics, on the dog-days he spread a large white handkerchief over the back of his head to protect his neck and held it in place with a grey top-hat, his normal headwear. His moustache was the soft billowy affair of the Victorians and even in old age he did not lose his hair which was pure white and so soft and fine that it looked more like the spinnings of the silkworm than human growth. His eyes were pale blue, rather yellow where they should have been white, and they had an unforgettable expression of dignity and disdain—though disdainful he never appeared in word or deed. He was extremely deaf for many of his last years and his sense of taste vanished. 'What is this I'm eating, Katie?' he asked my grandmother—it was rhubarb and custard—casting that strange, sad, lack-lustre glance at her. A sudden rift might come in his deafness and the same glance was turned on me as I chattered away to Grannie: 'In my youth "awful" was applied only to the Deity.'

I remember one conversation between us earlier than this, before age and deafness shut him off. We were waiting for a very late Highland train at a country junction, a dozen or more, adults and children, and I began to worry and fuss about the train, partly from boredom, partly because I felt someone ought always to fuss about an unpunctual train. Suppose we missed the next connection! My grandfather led me aside and we walked up and down on the fine cinders at the far end of the platform. He reminded me that not many months earlier my canary had flown away and had been missing for several days, and I had been content after praying for his safety to worry no more about him but believe that he would be found. (And so he was, high in a tree at the Royal Asylum, a mile from our house.) Surely my faith would not break down now, just because the train was overdue. This little homily either soothed or shamed me into patience.

A few years later at West Linton near Edinburgh it was my grandfather's turn to fuss. My older sister Elsa and I left the picnic group in order to climb a very modest hill. We descended on the further side and walked round by a little valley to join the family again towards the end of the afternoon. Grandpapa had been anxious when we disappeared from sight and he took us to task. 'Don't you know', he said, 'that mountaineers always come down a mountain the same way as they go up?' For many years I clung to this one piece of mountaineering lore, until I realized that it was a fabrication of my grandfather's, invented on the spur of the moment to cover up his shame at his unnecessary anxiety.

All his letters show boundless affection and humanity and a generosity usually wildly beyond his means. Here is one which must have been written in 1899, just after my parents moved from Liverpool to Berwick, with Aunt Christina to help them.

Home Saturday 7.30

My dear Christina,

We have not had a really good letter from Berwick for a week or ten days—and we want to know so much. I was quite disappointed when I got home at 7 yday to find there was nothing and all day, for I am in the house with a very bad cold for me, I have watched every postman from the window with dismay when he passed.

I want to know about furniture Warrington and Jedburgh alike and how it all comes in and I like to imagine it all being put in place.

My dear old chest of drawers are going to you—they were my Mother's when she was a bride 70 years ago—you can get nothing like them made now—and they were mine specially after her death when I had her room —and all the other things.

I want to know definitely if Johnson did not send off his things last Friday for he absolutely told me they had gone. He is a humbug—my bookcase after being promised twice, now will not be here for another week, if then.

And has your Uncle Andrew said anything yet to John about £50 for his Library solely. Did John get my letter from St. Boswell's of last Tuesday.

The Samuelsons have come hopelessly to grief and Edward (of Hoylake you remember him and his nice wife at Bettys) has bolted after confessing that for years he has falsified the a/cs and made believe they were making profits while all the while they were having big losses. Perrin loses 7,000, Rayner 10,000, Latham 8,000, and many others in proportion. John will know all these —it is most pitiful. Much apparent success in business is explained in the long run.

Willie is better but very washed out.

Love from us all

Your aff
FATHER

Some very solid rather ugly bedroom furniture was being made for the Berwick manse by Johnson, a cabinet-maker in Warrington. Two beds, a wardrobe, and a dressing table with a number of drawers in it cost £16. My great-aunt Isabella had just died in Jedburgh and much of the furniture of the old family home was also

sent to Berwick. The bookcase for which my grandfather waited with such impatience was a fine mahogany
piece, twelve feet long and eight feet high with closed
cupboards in the lower part and even a little pull-out
desk. It caused his family immense expense and trouble
after his death, because of its size and their sentiments. It
was moved four times, to Scotland and back to England,
everywhere involving the removal of windows, crises
upon stairs, double tips to removing men, and a great
deal of rather acid family correspondence.

I am sure my grandfather felt sympathy over the long-
forgotten business disaster, which he recounts almost as
an afterthought in this homely letter (so much of which
might have been written in almost any century since
English could be written by ordinary people). Yet there
is a tiny note of satisfaction in his reference to 'apparent
success in business', for through most of his life success
had not been apparent, nothing had been very clear except his faith and optimism and his inability to lower the
standard of life at 18 Devonshire Road by so much as a
pat of butter. To his sons Willie and Thorburn, who
started in business with him, and were both fortunately
very much better business men, both the optimism and
the fixed standard of comforts must have been trying.
My father (after taking a London B.A.) left the family
business at twenty-one to read theology at Queen's
College in London and so being less involved found
it easier to take a lenient view. The score or so of
letters from his father which he had preserved almost all
contained a reference to a gift of furniture or money.
Sometimes the money was called a loan, but then a later
letter would turn it into a gift, and on every occasion
with what pleasure and eagerness it is sent, what regret

that it is not more, what assurance that if there are other moments of need in the future he can turn again to his parents. I believe that my father kept these letters partly as a record of all the money he had received from his father, in case at any time he could repay it. That never occurred, but during the second world war, when he had retired, my father taught Greek and History to evacuated Edinburgh schoolboys and with his earnings repaid to the Carnegie Trust all the grants which had been made to five of us towards university fees at Aberdeen. (University education in Scotland was practically free from 1901 through the gift of Andrew Carnegie.)

A little memoir which my father wrote in the last year of his life gives a description of my grandfather's career without too much stress on the darker side of it.

'My father' (so wrote *my* father) 'started as a West African merchant in 1858 when he went out to Calabar where the chief articles of export were then palm oil and kernels, followed later by a poor kind of rubber and ground nuts. After the Crimean War the loss of certain fats from Eastern Europe caused a rise in the price of oils, but after 1878 my father did not do so well, mainly, though not entirely due to the fact that he and his partner refused on conscientious grounds to sell rum and gin to the natives, and so deprived themselves of the large profits to be made from this. It must be admitted that his enterprising spirit led him into ventures by which losses were sustained often through too great trustfulness in the promise of others. As time passed he found himself forced to abandon the merchant's business, which demanded a fair flow of capital, for that of a colonial broker, in which commissions on the sale of West African produce on behalf of the merchants and a like percentage from the

British or continental buyer yielded a fairly steady income. This it did until the merchants merged themselves in an association in which they had their own brokers. Fortunately other developments partly filled the gap, but the old business was at an end.

'The story of his many schemes, carried on alongside this, is a record of dazzling hopes and bitter disappointments, the latter preponderating. In the grounds of a nursery gardener just round the corner from Devonshire Road he had a greenhouse built about the year 1880, in which were reared coffee plants from the berry he had brought from Liberia. [My grandfather in a letter speaks proudly of "the gigantic coffee of Liberia which under the guidance of Kew Gardens I discovered in Africa".] The plants were successfully sold to planters all over the world and he made over £1,500 in a year from them. Very different was another venture. One summer day when I was a schoolboy, he took me for an excursion to Burton Point, where a plan was being worked out to reclaim land from the tidal incursions of the Dee estuary. We walked along an embankment that had given much promise of success until a north-west gale with an exceptionally high tide broke through and undid months of toil and expense. Lack of capital prevented effective repairs being carried out. The dyke remains still, with its gap, and the spring tides creep up to within a few yards of the lawn of a country house which is the home of one of his granddaughters.

'Lead mines in Flintshire and the Isle of Man, gunpowder stores on a desolate bit of marshland near Helsby on the Mersey, manganese in North Wales, all these attracted his active brain, but the largest of all his interests was the development of the gold mines of West Africa.

Beyond question he did much to set this field in its true importance among the enterprises of the mining world. But his own share in it was dogged by misfortune. He made the initial sacrifice. He indicated where the wealth lay, warier men stepped in and reaped the reward which should have been his. During his years on the Coast my father had come into very friendly relations with Captain Burton, a companion of Speke in the search for the sources of the Nile, who was at that time consul in Fernando Po; though he well knew what an unpredictable character he was. In 1881-2 it was arranged for Burton and Commander V. Lovett Cameron, another famous African explorer who in 1875 had crossed Africa from East to West, to visit the Gold Coast and write up the gold prospects there. It must have been an expensive business and I hardly think that it justified itself financially. On landing in Liverpool when they returned, they made straight for Devonshire Road. It was a Sunday afternoon, not the time that my father welcomed such a call. I remember a curious scuffling delay at the gate when their cab drew up. Then Mrs. Burton, who had met her husband and Cameron in Liverpool, rushed up the garden path to warn Aunt Minnie. *Il est enivré*. (It was Cameron.) We children were told to remain in the dining-room until the unfortunate incident was closed by their departure. Some years after Commander Cameron stayed with us and we found him a singularly delightful guest, simple, homely and friendly.'

Among my grandfather's acquaintances during the adventurous years of West African trading was Ja-Ja, originally a slave, who founded a kingdom at Opobo in Eastern Nigeria and became—after my grandfather's time there—the trading magnate of those parts. Some of the white traders grew tired of his demands and roused the British Consul to apprehend him. He died in exile in the later eighties.[1] But about 1860 his name had been given to a boat used for collecting palm oil from the up-river stations and taking it to the African coast for tran-shipment. We were very familiar with the story of my grandfather's coming down to breakfast in a boarding house at Beaumaris in the summer of 1877, saying that he had heard the whistle of a steamer in the night which sounded exactly like the whistle of the *King Ja-Ja*. For the good reason, as it turned out, that the *King Ja-Ja* had been sent home to Liverpool as unsuitable for the rivers of Africa, and was carrying freight between Liverpool and Carnarvon.

'One day from our Manse windows at Berwick, a quarter of a century later,' wrote my father in his memoir, 'I saw a small coaster slip up the river on the rising tide to the quay. She had a familiar look. Something about her masts and her funnel set far back woke long dormant memories, and I said to myself "If this were 1877 and I in Beaumaris, I should say 'There goes the *King Ja-Ja*!' "' Going down to the quay, I looked for her name and there sure enough it was, "*King Ja-Ja*, Liverpool". She was still doing work, on the run between Newcastle and Leith.' Some years later she ran ashore near St. Abb's Head and became a total wreck.

My grandfather carried on some shreds of his old romantic business in a single room in the office of an-

---

[1] For these facts about Ja-Ja I am indebted to an article by Mr. Giles Romilly called 'The Oil Rivers in the 19th Century', published in Number 229 of *Progress*, the magazine of Lever Brothers and Unilever Limited, Winter 1950–1. I came upon it quite accidentally.

other firm until he was over ninety. My Uncle Walter was alarmed one day to be rung up at his own office by a chemist in the city with the news that his father had fallen running to catch a bus. He hurried to the shop. 'Father, what have you been doing?' 'Why, fighting, of course,' said my grandfather, and he was none the worse for having forgotten his age so completely. But in the autumn of that year, 1926, he caught cold and went home from the office one day feeling not so well as usual. The next day pneumonia set in and on the following day he died. No news of his illness had reached me in Cambridge but I woke about six one morning weeping on my pillow after dreaming of my childhood. I had been in the back bedroom of the Aberdeen manse, the boys' room, and the wallpaper had a pattern of interlacing ribbon, as in our first years there, but so long since replaced that I had quite forgotten it. In my hands (in this dream) I held school exercise books of my brother Edward's and I read the essays he had written in a young sloping hand which altered completely when he grew up. My grief could not be explained by the dream itself and I was immediately persuaded that something must have happened to one of my sisters, and waited in apprehension for a letter from home. When it came with the news that my grandfather had died about six o'clock that morning of my dream I was both relieved and puzzled. It seemed strange that I should have a telepathic dream and weep so hard when I was perfectly resigned to losing my grandfather, as any sensible grandchild of so old and deaf a man should be. Another quarter of a century passed before I began to understand how strong a link with my origins snapped at his death, and that there were sympathies which bound us, visible to him although not

46

to me. My father's little memoir gave me a frame of the old man's life and later on I had access to the box of his letters to my father. One of these, very much longer and more formal than the others, was in part an apologia of his business failures and struggles, but it opened with the promise now to explain a recent escapade, in the previous summer of 1912. He had then been staying with Sir Robert Laidlaw at Wauchope on the Borders, near his birthplace and early home in Jedburgh, and went off by himself to climb Wolflee. He was seventy-six and had suffered a good deal from gout, and at Wolfhopelee he fell lame and allowed himself to be mounted on a quiet cob (although it was fifty years since he had ridden any sort of horse) and go up the hill in the company of the farmer.

This was his explanation. In 1846 or 1847, when he was a boy of eleven or twelve, he set out one day to walk from his Uncle John Telfer's farm, Braidhaugh in Rule Water,[1] to his Uncle Andrew Common at West-sheils far up Jed Water. He walked about half a mile along the highway which leads into England by the famous Note o' the Gate, and then turned off to the left up the old drove road which leads over the eastern shoulder of Wolflee into Jed Water. It was a perfect June morning, giving 'to simple existence a joy of life which craved for nothing more'. (His language has the delicate quality of one of the older hymn-writers.) When the boy approached the highest point of the road, he sat down to rest and enjoy the familiar view. To the south lay the noble mass of Carter Fell and below him to the east the valley of the Jed with nothing between but one rugged

[1] A farm locally known as *Spain*, not far from another called *Africa*.

47

solitary remnant of the great forest of earlier centuries. Beyond the valley and stretching far into the distance he saw the Cheviots themselves, moor, hill and valley, fold upon fold, tranquil and proud in the morning sunlight. The stillness was broken only by the bleating of sheep or the distant bark of a shepherd dog. In his letter my grandfather does not say what thoughts passed through his mind, but from natural enjoyment of the day and scene his mood changed to one of deep solemnity, something that he had never known before. He felt compelled to kneel upon the *bent*, and kneeling there, much moved, he offered the service of his life to Christ, and then continued on his way. It was an experience that he shared with no one for sixty years, but for eight more years after 1846, while his home was still in Jedburgh, he frequently passed by the place and knew it by the solitary tree that stood below upon the hillside. Then he moved south and until 1912 the opportunity to revisit Wolflee had never occurred. In his letter he says that the oak tree no longer marked the place, but that he found it nevertheless.

Conversion was a word that he did not like, and in any case it is not the right word for such an experience coming to a boy already rooted and grounded in faith. This was something different from the conviction of sin or the acceptance of salvation, for which a preacher strives from a pulpit or the platform of a stadium. Such a revelation as my grandfather knew, no words can induce, as no words can describe it to any but those who know it already. A state of understanding scarcely connected with any personal emotions lights up the whole of life, and when it ebbs away, it becomes evident that nothing is at all as it was before. A very great flood has come and gone, destroying nothing, but leaving everything strangely altered. The case of Brother Lawrence is familiar; for him the sight of a tree in winter let in the flood. For Wordsworth it was the sunrise as he returned home from a dance; and let me quote the story of an old woman, undistinguished and forgotten, called Peggy Gilroy, who lived about my grandfather's time and on the Borders too. 'I was not much more than a bairn, it was the Sabbath morn, and I was sitting down upon a bank. It was early in the summer time, and I was looking down upon the small flowers and the little wee fiernies among the grass, and it came over me all at once that they were all His work; my eyes were filled with tears, and the thought of his love and goodness filled my heart, and the joy of that day has always remained with me.'[1] This seems the hall-mark of such an experience, that unlike the exultation of success or creation or of love consummated, unlike liberation from fear or sickness or poverty or prison, unlike any of the high moments that one can name, it departs leaving something more than memory behind. The peace and the awe seem perpetually fed from a secret spring.

If my father shared my grandfather's strain of mysticism, he also kept it secret and for even longer. In his memoir he mentions only the services of the Children's Special Service Mission on the beaches of Wales as influencing him in his decision to enter the Church. The religion that he preached laid more emphasis on history and character than on the less explicable side of man's relationship with his creator. Yet William James's *Varieties of Religious Experience* stood always on a shelf near

---

[1] From *Under a Border Tower* by Hastings Neville, rector at Ford in the time of Louisa Marchioness of Waterford.

his desk and was much studied by him. He also distrusted and disliked the quick conversions of the tent preacher and his methods of achieving them, and that may have led him to hide anything in his own experience which even remotely resembled such conversions. Yet at the time of my father's sudden and beautiful death, the barrier between the seen and the unseen, normally so impenetrable, seemed for a short time fragile and insubstantial, ready to drop at a touch.

I cannot finish this chapter about my grandfather without talking of another death still, that of his first wife, the mother of the five older children. At forty-three she developed diabetes, then incurable, and was at times not at all well, and yet her last illness seems to have been almost unexpected. She died at the age of forty-six, in April of 1880, leaving the young family (my father was thirteen and Thorburn, the baby, six) to be cared for by Aunt Minnie, one of my grandfather's six remarkable sisters. Two detailed accounts of her death have come down to us, one a long letter from my grandfather to Mrs. Carmichael,[1] and the other, shorter, in pencil on tiny sheets of paper, written by the fourth child Helen aged seven at the time. She wrote it secretly at intervals and finished it five years later, keeping it for many years under the lining paper of one of the drawers of the chest in her bedroom. She made a little holland case to hold it and preserve it, and this was still among the papers in a tin doll's portmanteau which she handed over to me in her old age when her sight had gone. When I had looked through the papers she spoke shyly of the memorandum in the holland case. Helen alone had been sufficiently

[1] The mother of Amy Carmichael of Dohnavur, missionary and writer.

composed to speak when the children trooped in to kiss their mother good-bye, and had said 'Good-bye, Mamma' in her clear little voice, hiding from everyone her sense of the magnitude of the disaster. Even the others, less composed at the time, were considered by their father as 'strangely unbereft'. 'Children's sorrow is soon over,' he wrote to Mrs. Carmichael. But to us of the third generation it was clear that this sudden bereavement affected them deeply. Their mother had been about the house almost as usual even the day before, and although my grandfather had been up tending her all night, it was only when he drew the blinds at five in the morning (on a raw, wet April day) that he saw unmistakably that she was dying. Some hours of acute suffering followed. The family doctor called every half-hour. In the early afternoon she sank into a coma and died during the night.

Although my father never mentioned it, we knew that this dire memory never passed from his mind for long. If it was quite unavoidable for him to speak of his mother, he did so, but in a voice of extreme quietness and reverence. We knew from Aunt Christina that when she was sent up to his bedroom on the morning of April 5th to tell him that his mother had not lived through the night, he was sitting on the end of his bed, and fell backwards, like the high priest Eli sitting by the gate of Shiloh when he heard that the Ark of the Lord was taken. The idea that death could take a good and beloved mother with so many children still depending on her, frightened us greatly all through our childhood, the more so that so much silence and mystery surrounded it. The facts were sad enough but if we had known them it might have alarmed us a little less, and the gulf between us and our father and grandfather might have been bridged while they were still alive. When at last my grandfather's letter to Mrs. Carmichael came into my hands, and Aunt Helen's childish record, I felt thankful that at last my forebears had received me into the confidence of their woe. My grandfather—it must be clear already—was a very warm-hearted and emotional man. He held, with the Greeks, that no man need be ashamed of tears. 'Papa groaned so and said "My God, My God" at dinner,' wrote Helen in her secret notebook. As he sat by his wife after the children had made their last visit, too heart-broken to do anything but stroke her hand, Willie, aged eleven, came back into the room and first begged him to read the Twenty-third Psalm to his mother, and then himself read it in a clear and controlled voice, and followed it with some verses from the fourteenth chapter of St. John's Gospel. Their own distress was increased by this revelation of feeling beyond anything that they had conceived in Papa. It may be that a resolution never to be so defenceless themselves formed a shell over the naturally soft hearts of the elder ones, for all of them grew up far more reserved than their father. In the next century it was to become much easier and more common for people to discuss marriage and birth, and much more difficult for them to talk naturally of death in its personal aspect. The way in which neighbours crowded into the afflicted house and the whole household came into my grandmother's bedroom, weeping, praying, bidding her farewell; the frankness with which my grandfather told her that she was dying (she said 'with a distinct flash of surprise and pain on her face "Oh you don't think so".'): all this has been out of fashion a long time now.

When he conducted the morning service my father always prayed for those who through fear of death walked all their lives in the shadow. The possibility of a similar ordeal when the time came for my mother to go too, or for himself—that could never be brushed aside. But it happened quite differently. As a tree may fall on a still day, no one can say why, so he went off to preach on a June morning of hot bright sunshine and fell dead a stone's throw from the church. This very good old man —he was eighty-three—still strong and full of vigour, at a signal like the touch of a hand on his arm, stepped out of life. Among those letters of his father's already mentioned and a few other papers, we found a note headed Christmas Day 1877. 'To our dear good first born. Your Mama and I present you with this Silver Watch with the prayer that when time to you is no longer you will have entered the land where the sun shall no more go down.'

CHAPTER THREE

Irish Ancestors

When Edward was ten and I was six, my mother took us with her to visit the Irish grandparents at Fort Etna in County Limerick. Yda, a dear plump little girl not yet three, was left in charge of Aunt Christina with the other grandparents at 18 Devonshire Road. Both aunt and niece had strong views, so a fearful battle of wills raged at first. Yda liked freshly laundered damask table napkins to cover her doll as it slept. The aunt removed them and substituted blue check dusters, but as soon as her back was turned Yda threw the duster in a corner and fetched a clean table napkin from the drawer. I suspect that Aunt Christina won this war, for as we entered the house on our return from Ireland, Yda was plodding sideways, a step at a time, down the stairs, and when she saw it was her mother in the hall, she burst into loud and bitter retrospective howls—to Aunt Christina's great indignation.

We were nearly a month in Ireland, and the month was June. As the train plodded through the quiet countryside on the long journey to Limerick, the air seemed to get warmer and softer and sweeter all the way. The sweetness came from the roses and honeysuckle frothing over the palings at the tiny railway stations. When at last we reached Limerick the jaunting car met us, familiar from drawings in *Punch* and my mother's tales of driving to church with her feet squeezed into her sister Mary's cast-off boots. My mother pointed out the landmarks as we went along and we caught her excitement and felt that we too were coming home after a long exile. Here were the park gates and the lodge, and then the long drive up between the paddocks to the garden and the roomy old house whose one authentic ghost stayed considerately outside, merely driving up to the front door in an invisible coach once a year. Only Aunt Lucie lived at home with the grandparents, so the house had many deserted and half-furnished rooms. No one used the nursery which had figured in so many of my mother's reminiscences, but it was very interesting for us to examine the little cupboard where the Irish nursemaid threw the tea-leaves and scraps into a bowl. Once the big house-dog who knew the nurse's habits had come to my mother asleep in bed and nosed her with his muzzle all wet and messy with tea-leaves. Her yells had brought the grown-ups, and afterwards the cupboard was less smelly. And no one now used the schoolroom, where Miss Mac-quillan, tougher than any of the English governesses, had ruled for five long years. There my mother and her three sisters stood every day to repeat their lessons with a sprig of holly under the chin and arms curled round the arms of a backboard. If hearts were in stomachs, nothing could show with such a posture. Miss Macquillan sat with all the lesson books open and neatly arranged beside her, the largest at the bottom and the smallest at the top, irrespective of subject. Aphra, the youngest, sometimes became quite dumb during her examination, whereupon Miss Macquillan would say 'The little bird that can sing and won't sing must be MADE TO SING.' And Aphra was sent to bed, although there is no record that it loosened her tongue. It was easy for us to imagine this and much more. We could picture my mother and her sisters collecting their work-bags in the evening and trooping down to the dining-room for an hour. The eldest son, Arthur, sat by the fire with his father and his step-mother and his own sister Lucie, and if Arthur happened to be in a good mood the group round the fire conversed. But always the little girls round the big table sat silent with their needlework until the hour struck for bed. Then they rose and said good night and retired to an even greater trial of courage in the schoolroom where the governess awaited them. If the day had passed well, if the little birds had sung, the governess offered her cheek to be kissed (like Mrs. Wilfer's, 'as sympathetic and responsive as the back of the bowl of a spoon'). If it had been a bad day—and no one could certainly foresee Miss Macquillan's judgment—a cold hand was dangled for the offending child to touch, and an equally cold voice said 'Good night'. We thought our own lot much happier, and yet we had our troubles too at Fort Etna, for we slept with my mother in the best spare room, which was the largest room that I had ever slept in. The curtains over the high windows were heavy and dark. In the night when such curtains are pulled so that not even a pencil line of starlight shows, how can a child be sure, waking to a great stillness, that it has not been buried alive or fallen through the abyss to a place unknown? And by day the big yard behind the house alarmed us, by reason of the dogs and the horsey smells, and unfamiliar people coming and going.

Beyond the yard lay the best place of all, and fortunately we did not need to cross the yard to reach it, but could go round the house by a dark path through the shrubbery. There we came to a door in the north wall of the garden and passed from the shade into the heat and brightness, to the flowers and fruit and vegetables separated by deep box hedges and the ripe cherries hanging on the immense stone walls. At the far end there was an arched opening which led not out into the world again but into an even more still and sacred place, just as big as the upper garden and walled to the same impressive height, the orchard itself, where the shade of the trees and the coolness of the deep grass rewarded us for having come so far. At the very end of the orchard was an old stone well with hart's-tongue fern growing from the cracks between the stones.

Although to a child born and brought up in Berwick-on-Tweed an ancient stone wall was as familiar as a loaf of bread, yet the wall of the garden at Fort Etna seemed to have a special importance. No boundary had ever been so tremendous for me and the tops of the group of pine trees over the far west wall belonged to an unknown and unimaginable landscape. In those days I required no knowledge of its history to quicken my reflections, but now I should dearly like to know if the stones of the walls came from the ruins of a castle (Fort Etna—such an odd name for a gentleman's house) and the old well once supplied the garrison.

In spite of my feeling about the country over the wall, I knew very well that the railway to Limerick ran through the fields just a short walk from the house. The road from the village of Patrickswell to the gates of the park crossed the rails, and that was where the station

ought to have been built. But by that time Uncle Arthur
had moved to Attyflin, the next estate and the home of
his wife, Mary Massy Westropp. As solicitor to the railway company he had no difficulty in arranging for the
station to be further from the village and within a comfortable distance of his own front door. As for my
grandfather he merely walked across the paddock to the
north of the house and waved his stick to the engine-
driver if he wished to board a train and go to Limerick.

At the time of this visit in 1907 my grandparents were
leading rather a straitened existence. My grandfather,
already eighty-six, had retired from the family firm, and
that and all the property owned by the family was in
Uncle Arthur's hands. He made an allowance to his
parents and they eked out the money by selling fruit
from the garden. All that my grandfather possessed was
left to Arthur with an understanding that he would give
a suitable share to the other children. But like Mr. John
Dashwood and others before and since, he found the
difficulties of deciding what was suitable too great. He
did not live many years after his father and left everything to his childless wife. This story was often mentioned as a major family scandal, specially in our branch
of it, where even the penny for the Dutch doll could not
be spared without thought. But long after this when
Arthur's widow died, it was found that she had left half
of her rather shrunken fortune to the three sisters-in-law
still surviving—the White girls—by this time girls in
their late seventies and early eighties, but by no means
too senile to know what to do with a little money.

But let me just turn over the precious crumbs of
memory that are all I have left of that first visit in 1907.
Aunt Lucie gave me a shell lined with pale pink as

smooth as satin as far as my smallest finger could reach or
my curious eye peer, round that bend leading to places
that were really very secret indeed and must be so for all
time. My grandmother gave me a china mug with a gay
Irish cock painted on it, from which I drank milk so new
that it was unpleasantly warm. We fed upon three-
cornered brown loaves baked in the kitchen, and boiled
eggs so fresh that a little milky fluid rested on the yolk.
The butter too was home-made and a robin used to fly
about the dining-room and sit upon my grandfather's
hand, eating butter off the blade of his knife. The wood-
pigeon called all day from the paddock: 'Tak two coos,
Taffy, tak two coos, tak!' Outside the dining-room window there must have been a chaffinch's nest, for the cock
chaffinch never stopped its cheerful, superficial rigmarole
from morning to evening. On the other side of the front
garden by the drawing-room windows grew a fine
weeping ash which we pretended was a tent until the
rain came, and then we went to play in the mountains of
straw in the great barn.

Three years after this first happy visit, my mother took
me to Fort Etna again. Edward was too old to be permitted to miss school and Yda came with us instead. My
mother went to prodigious trouble with our wardrobes
and sat at the sewing machine through the whole of our
last night before travelling, making us full-skirted frocks
finely striped in red and white. Sometimes our dresses
were smocked by my mother, or embroidered on the
yoke, and she chose soft, warm materials such as nuns'
veiling or nainsook. I remember one pair of dresses (we
were always dressed alike) of soft white material covered
with tiny pink rosebuds, with pockets made of the same
material, a gathered and frilled pocket such as Lucy

Locket lost, dangling on ribbons from the yoke. The short full sleeves were caught up with more ribbons on the shoulder.

After her vigil at the sewing machine my mother endured another vigil on the boat. She had left the porthole open against the advice of the stewardess and in the night the sea romped through, soaking her bed beneath the porthole although it did not reach me and Yda in the two opposite bunks. In her distaste for troubling anyone merely for her own comfort, she did not call the stewardess nor move me and Yda into one bunk. She tipped the mattress up to drain and wrapped herself in a coat and rug and sat until morning on the hard frame of the bunk. I was restless and rather sea-sick and woke many times, always to see her there by the meagre light from a lamp in the passage outside, a patient, bowed figure, with long fair hair loose over her shoulders and her sleepy head dropping towards her breast. My mother had one very trying fault. She was unable to draw the line in self-abnegation, and so defeated her own purpose, giving at times more distress than happiness to others. Nor could she see that it might be pleasurable for her children to be kind to her; pleasure of that sort was her prerogative and hers alone. This brought about much teasing and argument, twisting and evasion. No one ever flew more brazenly in the face of logic than she. But in the end her body furnished a rigorous argument of its own, and when she had no alternative but to accept our ministrations, she did so with charming grace and humour.

This second visit to Ireland took place in April, partly in order that we should see cowslips. Primroses were plentiful round both Berwick and Aberdeen, but the more beautiful and sturdier cowslip was unknown to

us and its incomparable marmalade smell a wonderful
new experience. My mother showed us how to make
cowslip balls, and hung them on ribbons round our
necks. We ran about the golden meadows, picking more
and more, with our cowslip balls bouncing against our
stomachs or flying behind over our shoulders. But soon
after we arrived Edward VII died. My grandfather, now
eighty-nine, took the news badly, and sat brooding by
the fire, overcome by foreboding. His memories went
back to the reign of George IV, through many dark times
in Irish history. In July 1849, during the Famine and
Plague, his elder brother Richard had been shot dead on
his own doorstep and for many years the iron bars had
been fixed across the doors and windows of Fort Etna at
sunset, and the loaded gun put ready. Now with the
death of a king whom he trusted his hopes of peace in
the future vanished, but the women of the house said
that his age and approaching death had cast a gloom over
him. I peeped into the dining-room before running out
to play, and saw him sitting there quite still and silent, the
tall, fine old man with his white beard, and an idea that
life might be very unlike what I knew and believed
flashed into my mind and out again.

A few days later however he had thrown off his
depression and taught me the answer to my first riddle:
'Which is the oldest of the trees?' A very dusty and
obstinate donkey used to be brought round from the
farm every morning for us to ride up and down the long
drive to the park gates. My grandfather fetched a sheepskin for a saddle and while we waited for the donkey we
sat on the sheepskin on the stone steps leading to the front
door, talking together about pleasant simple things. Once
he had bought a very young donkey, 'a little ass', from a

beggar woman for a penny. But I was not entirely happy for all the time moisture gathered in a clear drop at the end of his nose and fell into the sheepskin just about the place where I should soon be pressing my bare knee. Sometimes he caught it with his handkerchief and brought out a little proverb or quotation about old men's noses, but mostly he did not seem aware of it.

The attitude towards us at Fort Etna was very much more indulgent than at 18 Devonshire Road; we were not looked upon as little children with characters to be formed so much as a source of pleasure to adults, and reasons for complimenting my mother who was the apple of their eyes. When Yda and I, back at the Scottish manse, used to vex my mother in any way, her trump card was to remind us that our Irish grandfather thought us 'everything that little girls should be'. My grandmother's face returns to me even now, smiling with tender amusement as I lean against her and explain something very complicated and important. (She wore a tiny cap of lace with black velvet bows in it.) She turns to my mother, saying in her melancholy sweet Irish voice: 'Now listen to the little creature, Lily.'

My mother could just remember her own maternal grandmother, Anne Locke, as she was born, descended from a relative of John Locke the philosopher. This great-grandmother of mine was dreadfully paralysed by an illness in her early thirties, but when her hands were lifted on to the table she could write with an elegance and regularity singular even in those days. She also embroidered texts and mottoes on perforated cardboard to make cases for sticking-plaster and book-marks. Fifty years after her death, and even seventy years, her name comes up in family letters with references to the gaiety and charm and the simple holiness of her character. My mother was very proud to be called after her and prized her miniature, and handed down both her variation of the name and the miniature to me. From time to time the Locke features appear in the family and become noticeable as age fines down the flesh: the long nose and deep-set eyes, the characteristic moulding of temple and cheek-bone. In my mother in old age the resemblance to the Locke of Kneller's portrait struck even those who knew nothing of the relationship.

Aunt Lucie, who was Uncle Arthur's own sister and the only daughter by my grandfather's first beautiful and lamented wife, figured in so many of my mother's stories, that we met her with particular awe and interest when we went to Ireland. She had been a beauty and a flirt, dressed fashionably and even played tennis. It was for Lucie that the latest music was ordered from Dublin and she played on the piano in the drawing-room, while the other girls practised in the schoolroom. But my mother used to borrow Lucie's pieces when she was out and learn them in secret, and thirty or forty years later when the mood took her she would sit down and play Weber's Invitation to the Waltz. Whatever we were doing at the time we stopped and rushed to stand by the piano and listen. After knowing the Lucie of my mother's memories, it was disconcerting to meet Aunt Lucie and find her a prim little lady in black silk with a watch-chain on her bosom. She became bedridden some years before she died and lived on, writing incessantly to her sisters begging for their prayers, very tired of life. The curtains of the room where she lay were always drawn and she allowed no light but that of candles lest anyone should see what time had done to her appearance. I inherited a leather writing-desk which had belonged to her, a finely made and fitted piece of work though black and severe. On its tablets were faint rubbed-out traces of addresses and notes in her handwriting, and some influence of heat or light made them grow legible after I had used the desk some years. On one tablet she had written: 'Past—I haven't future.' When my mother played to us Aunt Lucie's pieces or told us about life in the seventies at Fort Etna, we felt that these memories of her childhood were almost intolerably sweet and precious to her. We never knew what it was that gave such distant times a scent that could survive, like the scent in the leaves of pressed verbena which we kept in our Bibles in church, strong and aromatic when the leaves themselves were almost too dry and brittle to stand being moved to a new page.

My mother belonged to a different stratum of civilization from my father, earlier, simpler, more inbred and credulous. He was aware from early childhood of foreign parts and other nations. The Gold Coast was almost as real to him as the coast of North Wales, and at school he was soon eagerly learning the histories of Greece and Rome and studying the literature of those countries, until the classics became part of his daily reflections. My grandfather in Ireland had a little copy of *Pliny's Letters*, which perhaps he pushed in his pocket when he went to the office in Limerick, or rode about the estate, but that must have been a private, casual interest. The women at home, mending and sorting linen, picking flowers and preserving fruit, told and retold all the stories of their Irish relatives, the love affairs and the unhappy marriages, the royal rows and tender reconciliations, the calamities, deaths, births, hauntings, illnesses and miraculous escapes.

Their voices sounded soft, plaintive and lilting as they
flowed easily on, each speaker catching some of the in-
spiration of a ballad-monger, and the audience always
happy and absorbed to hear again the familiar tales. After
religion, it was what mattered most, the essence of life,
how people of their own blood had lived and felt and
met their private fates. My mother carried the custom on
with us as children. She sat on our beds in the evening
and we listened with delight to the history of Aunt
Nanno's father, with his big house in Merrion Square,
his eleven children and his fits of madness—when he
believed himself to be a frog; to the tale of the liaison of a
brow-beaten cousin with a gipsy woman, which cul-
minated with the birth of a baby girl under a hedge:
whereupon the father put the baby in a carpet bag and
brought it to his sisters to rear for him. With even keener
interest we heard my mother's memories of her court-
ship and marriage, for without those events our own
appearance upon earth lay open to the gravest doubt.
'And suppose', I used to say, 'you had married Mr. Mont-
morency and not Father, would I have been me?' A great
deal was left to the imagination. 'Well, my dears, that
was all,' she would say as we clamoured for particulars.
'He never saw her again.' Or—'They used to say that
she never smiled again.' Nothing was ever touched up
but all handed down with the starkness common to the
folk legend. Occasionally there popped out, like a trace
of red flannel under a silk skirt, a phrase or word from
the Irish maids or gardeners or grooms. Simple psycho-
logical ailments had Irish names—Lurragathawn Fever—
a horrid lassitude—and the Pheebeen, the opposite afflic-
tion. It makes the cows stampede in hot weather and
human beings move the furniture about or start to clean

E   65

the house when it was very well just as it was before.
The darkest of all curses was the Curse of Cromwell (a
particular hero of my father's), and when very old my
mother unexpectedly informed me that the Devil had a
mother called Yerra. I had lost a diamond from a ring,
and Yerra, the Devil's mother, was to blame.[1] Very little
however of the rich and supple talk of the true Irish came
through to us, and it surprised me when some time in the
early thirties of this century my mother wrote asking me
to send her a copy of James Joyce's *Anna Livia Plurabelle*,
not the sort of book that found its way naturally to the
Aberdeen manse. I do not know how she had gained the
idea that it was for her, but she found no mysteries in the
text and through it she heard to her amazement and
delight for the first time since childhood, the authentic
voices from below stairs.

I do not doubt that the influence of Irish speech—the
skill of the Irish in their use of English—helped to give
her the soft yet lively grace which adorned her talk and
made her letters so unlike any others that we ever received. 'Oh the cream has gone from my post now,' said
Aunt Aphra when my mother died—and this was the
more remarkable since she had been too blind to re-read
anything that she wrote for the last twenty months of her
life.

We believed many contrary things about my mother
and her origins. On the one hand we suspected that
Anglo-Irish Protestants were intruders and not the
real thing. Much might be laid at their doors; perhaps

[1] My friend Mgr Browne offers the brilliant explanation that to
break her children of the vulgar exclamation Yerra (in Irish a con-
traction of '*A dhia Ara!*'—'O Goddess Ara!') my grandmother said:
'Yerra is the Divil's mother.' Cf. 'Who is *she*—the cat's aunt?'

they even constituted the Curse of Cromwell. Yet we imagined that Roman Catholics were more dangerous than the heathen themselves, and that Irish Roman Catholics were particularly unreliable. But again, there was no doubt that my mother was Irish, for my father was constantly saying so, half in amusement and half in despair, and all the Irish, whether Catholic or Protestant, whether descended from the ancient Celts or from English adventurers, were always irrational, impulsive and crazy and unable to understand the jokes in *Punch*. But we did not worry about these contradictions and we did not dream of criticizing the social fabric which yielded so much comfort and beauty to my mother's family and all its ramifications in the south of Ireland.

A picture of how these Irish ancestors lived in 1839 (the year John O'Leary was born) survives in three combined letters which alone of many thousands (so it seems) escaped destruction and was eventually passed to me by one of my aunts. Perhaps it was preserved for the sake of the seal, or for the gayness of Nan who filled up all the space on the folded sheet that her father and brother had left. Or it may be that the reference to Paddy Daly and the key caught the eye of a reader rummaging through family papers, and it was sent to Mary or Lil, who were old enough to remember some talk of Paddy.

The first letter on the sheet is written by my great-grandfather, who was born in 1775, to his wife dearest Moll, thanking God and telling her that he had arrived safe in Dublin with no more than a shower on the Couragh all the way. He was visiting his son Edward, my grandfather, who seems to have been studying in Dublin. On the back of this short note Edward writes that he hopes himself to be home in a week; he is grateful for the shirts and will see about the wool for Nan and sends his love to all. At home (that was Abbeyville, a house near Croom in County Limerick) Nan takes up her pen late at night to pass these letters on and give the news from home to her sister Bessie[1] staying with a Sayers relative in Limerick.

Dearest Bessie (she wrote),

We got this letter from Papa today and you will see by it he will not be down as soon as he expected. Ma sends it as it will be only 3^d and will save uneasiness.

The bedstead came *quite* safe and seems to be a very nice one and so large too. Ma will get Joany Crowe to come and make the curtains. Ma was at Lemonfield to-day—no one at home but Mrs. Brown the ladies were gone to Lim^k & Eddy went. Mrs. Brown was very kind but she is very feeble—just recovering from a heavy nervous attack. Ma did not go to Mary Ville as she thought it might look as if she wanted to pry about Miss Conoly. Ma likes the *Cock*—thanks for the cake it was very nice and many thanks to Mag for the salmon but she is sorry Mag bought it as Papa was not here. Ma wants you to buy 2 squares of muslin for cravats for Papa—they need not be fine *she* says—but *I* say do not have them too coarse. I locked up all the things but could not find what Miss Westropp sent at all.

I hope to send my pet some flowers whatever day the car goes for Papa. I am so glad Mag's foot is better. Dick said you went to drive on Thursday. How very cheap Ed. Hewson got the lodge. Thanks for the bread. I had a note from Aunt Sally—she said Dawson Massy is not as

[1] Bessie afterwards married William Fry, founder of the firm of Dublin solicitors. Nan married an O'Keeffe.

well as he was. Paddy Daly had not the key of the stable
at all the day he was in Lim^k it was a man that was getting
mortar had it open & since the time that the key was
broken that they said he broke it he has had very little to
do with it since. I wrote this in the dark can you make it
out. Thanks to whoever sent the little pots. I hope Maria
liked the flowers—we are all quite well thank God & I
drive for an hour every day before breakfast. We will
send Mag the papers—would the Mails do for I send the
Standards to Ed.

All the comfortable ways of a landed family uninten-
tionally listed, including the little difference of view
about Papa's cravats. But it is my great-aunt's spurt of
indignation over Paddy Daly and the key that makes me
love her, the implication in 'they said' and the lines under
at all, and the picture she gives me of that proud servant
with the blood of the ancient Irish poets in him, who will
have as little as possible to do with the locking of his
master's stable since the row and the injustice that was
done him.

There was no simple way out of the tangle of Irish
politics and I cannot imagine that any of my ancestors
wanted to find a hard way out. Gifts to the more needy
or importunate peasants eased the conscience a little, and
however incredible the poverty, the charity too belongs
to another age than ours. No beggar was ever turned
away from my grandmother's door. The maids themselves grew impatient with her bounty and one young
hussy ordered the old woman at the kitchen door to hold
up her apron and then poured a bowl of hot soup into
her lap. Even eighty years ago no one was allowed to
insult the staff with impunity. There was no fear of a

servant's giving notice, but my grandmother had strong principles, and when Aunt Aphra as a very small girl had been rude to the cook she was deprived of all the pleasures of life until she agreed to apologize. She descended at last to the kitchen holding her mother's hand, and face to face with Cook made her solemn apology—'*I begive you Biddy.*'

NOTE ON THE NAME FORT ETNA

In my mother's family it was assumed that the name Etna was borrowed from Mount Etna, and 'fort' lost most of its significance by being linked in this borrowing. Helena Shire has, however, thrown out the interesting suggestion that Fort Etna is an English rendering of the Dun of Etain. The story of Etain, wife of Midhir and afterwards of Eochaid Feidlech, High King of Ireland, is in Lady Gregory's *Gods and Fighting Men*. This is also the Princess Edane whose story Mary Bruin reads in the old book out of the thatch in *The Land of Heart's Desire*.

CHAPTER FOUR

Living in Aberdeen

My story broke off at the end of Chapter One to talk of grandparents, and now after skipping backwards and forwards over a century, I want to take up the threads again with our departure from Berwick-on-Tweed for Aberdeen, in the spring of 1908. My father had preceded us by some days, and Edward went off to Uncle Norman and Aunt Helen in Glasgow in order to have his tonsils removed in their house. I did not know Glasgow, but had a symbolic picture in my mind's eye of an immense sooty pair of pince-nez (the glasses of Glas-gow). This served me well for many years whenever the city was mentioned in conversation, and the report given by Edward of his experiences did nothing to enlarge or improve it. He was allowed nothing to drink and not even a grape to suck for many hours after the operation, and suffered horribly from thirst, blaming Aunt Helen who nursed him, although I am sure that she was following the instructions of her doctor husband. We both knew that if my mother had been there twenty doctors would not have prevented her doing something to assuage his thirst.

The manse at Aberdeen was not quite ready for us, and my mother and Yda and I were given hospitality by the Abernethys at Ferryhill Cottage, not far from the successful iron foundry owned by Mr. Abernethy. Ferryhill Cottage made a deep impression. The copper cans of hot water shone so very brightly, and came scalding hot to our comfortably furnished bedroom. When I sat upon the floor lacing up my long black boots, the thickness and warmth of the carpet surprised me, so did the admiration of Miss Minnie Abernethy at my ability to lace my own boots. 'Indeed,' said my mother, 'who should lace them if she didn't herself?'

Mr. Abernethy and his two sisters—they were all quite unmarried—baffled me by their appearance at that time and for long after. Their stout stocky figures and weather-beaten leonine faces made a wall which I could never see over. I was almost as far from knowing what they really were as from realizing that Glasgow was made up of buildings. But their kindness and goodness and integrity, which I ignored at the time in my preoccupation with their appearance, was still a warm and living flame when at last I came to my senses, long after I had left home, long after they were dead. And so it was with my ideas and memories of many of my father's congregation.

The manse, 5 Westfield Terrace (afterwards given the much less distinguished number of 10), was a pleasant, sunny, semi-detached house built of rusticated granite blocks with dressings of freestone. A small peaked turret sprouted out between the two houses and the little dormer windows in the attics had window-panes shaped like shamrock leaves. The style was neo-Gothic at its best, and the turret made a charming addition to a bedroom in the house of our neighbours, the Lillies (whose son

Robert later became a great admirer of W. G. Gillies and collected many of his pictures). We felt aggrieved about the turret as the Lillies seldom used it and thought it rather superfluous. To sit there on a moonlight night looking out on the three sickly cypress trees that grew in our shrubbery would have made me very happy.

The manse was much colder than Ferryhill Cottage, being so much taller, in fact for warmth and comfort there was little to choose between it and the Berwick manse. Upstairs in the centre of the house a boxroom had been converted into a bathroom, lit and ventilated by a skylight at the top of a high shaft, a skylight which either would not shut or was never shut on principle. The snow whirled very freely down the shaft, but never in such a way as to prevent much of the warmth from the rooms below from going up it. The bath itself was not very useful. The hot-water system was weak, always under repair but never quite repaired, and if by any chance the kitchen range did succeed in heating the water, the paint in the bath melted and came off on one's body. We therefore used it mainly for cold baths which were traditional in my father's family. The bath was often filled the night before to save time in the morning, and the musical, sad little sound of an occasional drop from the tap landing in the bath full of water would punctuate the silent stretches of the night. It was quiet within and quiet without. Sometimes a goods train shunted in the yards in the centre of the town, or long before dawn my heart would be troubled by the forlorn crowing of a cock in a farmstead away on the edge of the country.

In the bathroom beside the big bath and immediately under the shaft stood a zinc sitz bath filled for each of us every morning with hot water boiled in a huge kettle on

73

a gas-ring. After soaping in the sitz bath, lying with my head on the short slope and my legs up the back in order to get the largest area of body under water, I jumped into the icy-cold water in the big bath to rinse off the soap. It is usual to insist that these almost forgotten customs insured health, but in fact Yda and I were both delicate in one way or another, inclined to have shocking colds, influenza, rheumatic pains, headaches and chilblains. We did escape some of the usual infectious diseases of childhood, such as measles and mumps, to suffer inordinately when we caught them in middle age. My mother loved fresh air, partly because her sense of smell was exceptionally acute, and our friends used to say that her home could always be recognized from far away by the curtains like flags streaming from the open windows. We often woke to find ice on the glass of water at the bedside, and sometimes there was snow on the floor, slanting up incongruously against the pretty flowered paper under the window, like a Swiss spring scene. But the dining-room fire was always a magnificent blaze when we came down to breakfast, and the rows of boots warming in front of it were frequently in danger of being scorched. My mother particularly disliked putting our feet into cold shoes or boots, and in the Berwick days when I wore patent leather ankle-strap slippers, she used to light the gas jet above her bed, and carefully folding back the straps, hold each slipper in turn over the petal-shaped flame before quickly popping it on to my foot. But while she never approved of feeling cold, neither she nor anyone else knew quite how to distinguish between fresh air and a piercing draught.

The dining-room in the Aberdeen manse became our play-room in cold weather; nowhere else in the house was endurable except my father's study and the kitchen. Fortunately we had few of the toys and equipment of modern children to scatter around, rarely anything but dolls and soldiers, with hoops and skipping-ropes for the garden and the terrace. The dining-room provided a fine and monumental stage. Apart from one plush arm-chair all the furniture was mahogany—a large and noble sideboard from the Berwick manse; a dinner-wagon with three immense polished shelves which might have been hitched to a train but could never be used as a wagon in any ordinary house. The dining-room table, extendable (and often extended) with extra leaves in the middle, stood on two mahogany pillars rising from two platforms, each mounted upon four feet carved to resemble the huge paws of a mythical monster. The business of dusting their deep grooves was often neglected, but that did not matter much for the table was covered with a piece of thick mottled material with an edging of ball fringe. We played under the table a great deal since it was space that nobody else required, like the well between the cupboards of the sideboard. The well made a cave, the table a tent and the dinner-wagon, on which we climbed unforbidden and lay outspread, shoes, buttons and all, often served as a ship with three large berths. We fitted up the dining-room chairs as horses and chariots, and with this wealth of property and the run of my mother's wardrobe, it was easy to stage plays and charades from the Old Testament. Sometimes Aunt Christina obliged us by coming to watch and guess. Jael, the wife of Heber the Kenite, drove the tent nail through the temples of Sisera. Rahab let down the spies from the walls of Jericho. The women in the siege of Samaria argued which child should be eaten first. Nebuchadnezzar munched

75

grass. Ruth slept at the feet of Boaz. The widow of Zarephath made a little cake on her fire of sticks for the prophet Elijah. The Shunammite's son sneezed seven times, and when Balaam's ass spoke, we could use our real donkey's head, almost the most treasured thing in the house. It must have been made for Bottom and came to us from the Hodsons, our next-door neighbours in Berwick. I learnt to know and respect the density and weight and texture of our dining-room furniture as at Berwick I had grown familiar with the stones of the pier and the old walls. The stones were harder, and many of them were rough. One paid rather more dearly for a fall or a clumsy movement with stone than mahogany, yet I loved the stone better than the wood. It seemed entirely correct that our lives should be furnished in this solid fashion and our thoughts never drifted off to fancy anything lighter or softer within doors or without. To the modern child such an upbringing as ours might seem drab and uneventful. But I was hardly ever bored. Convalescing from influenza in 1918 I suffered from a sense of emptiness and flatness that was quite new to me. I climbed with my eyes the trellis of the pattern on my bedroom walls, like a weary fly searching for sustenance or entertainment, and thought this must be the first stage in madness. Normally my mind seemed to me like a bottomless rag-bag to a tireless maker of patchwork quilts, and time has added many odd snippets to the rag-bag yet taken nothing from my zest for matching and piecing.

All the houses in Westfield Terrace were very much alike architecturally, but I liked to visit our neighbours and study the slight differences, variations from the normal of the manse, and also to study the pictures on their walls, some of them even more crowded than our own with prints and etchings and water-colours. Of some prints we had a copy too, such as Holman Hunt's 'The Light of the World'; but we never possessed 'The Soul's Awakening' or 'When did you last see your Father?' I took for granted that 'The Light of the World' was a fine picture and that I liked it, but in fact I looked at it as little as possible. I asked no questions about this picture, yet seemed constantly to be hearing its meaning. On the other hand in my father's study hung a reproduction of Dürer's 'Knight, Death and the Devil' which stimulated my curiosity to a point of despair. The knight himself, noble and inscrutable, riding to a strange place indeed, but where, where? The trees and tangled shrubs, so alive; the dog, the horse and the devil, never perfectly separated, like so much that I saw about me in the world; and then far off the city on the hill, a vision that I believed with all my heart although I was not to see it with my waking eyes for nearly thirty years. I asked both my parents to tell me what it was all about, but they knew nothing at all. It had been given to them as a wedding present, rather to their surprise. The only other picture that I saw as a little girl which struck straight between the eyes hung to the right of the drawing-room mantelpiece at Mrs. Henderson's across the road: a water-colour copy of the head of Dante from Giotto's fresco in the Bargello in Florence. The portraits of Christ in our Bible pictures were idle ciphers by comparison. I had never seen such a face and felt again a piercing curiosity like a pain in my vitals, to know who it was and who had painted him and where and why.

I was born much too soon for any freedom to draw and paint myself as I wished, to see on paper the queer and beautiful shapes of things, some inside and some out-side my mind. At school I was early commended for the care with which I drew sea-shells and dusty white geometrical solids. As I grew older and moved to the Girls' High School flowers were added, and dead butter-flies, and once for variety a turnip. I do remember that turnip and wonder if any individual turnip has been remembered as long since evolution threw out the turnip. It was green near the top and had a strange resemblance to a clouded planet. On its eastern hemisphere lay a brown blotch just north of the equator. When I had finished putting all this on paper with my water-colours the art master came and looked over my shoulder and burst out laughing. He laughed so much that the tears came into his eyes and he had to blow his nose; then be-cause I looked puzzled and perhaps a little alarmed he explained that it was the best turnip he had ever seen, and to prove this he took four thumb tacks and pinned it up firmly on the blackboard. Much later at my next school the drawing mistress took a small group of the better pupils on sketching parties in summer. This was Miss Davidson, a gentle person with an eye for natural beauty, and she trained us to see the charm of the coun-try round Aberdeen. I learnt from her to do water-colour sketches of old bridges and cottages and country lanes in the meek style of many of my female ancestors. By that time I had accepted my inability to paint anything that really mattered.

As for the musical side of our education, someone was usually playing the piano, Mendelssohn's 'Spring Song' or the 'Watchman's Cry' by Grieg, and we all sang a great deal, solo or in unison, hymns and songs and ballads and nursery rhymes and ditties of every description. Hurdy-gurdies and martial bands, cornets, accordions, mouth organs and bagpipes kept up a sturdy racket around us, and we buzzed away ourselves on haircombs folded in tissue paper. Our heads stored hundreds of tunes but we knew very little about music. We had no radio and no gramophone, and never went to concerts or opera, in fact I did not hear an orchestra at all until I was over twelve. Then it was only a small and indigenous one, playing for a bazaar in one of the smaller halls adjoining Aberdeen Music Hall, but I was much excited. I wandered into the big hall and climbed among the empty seats and saw for the first time the huge rather shadowy mural paintings of the life of Orpheus by Douglas Strachan. All the time I could hear the orchestra playing, and there was Orpheus in the veils of the underworld with his hand upon his lute. A worshipping state of mind was engendered which returned whenever I visited the hall even if the occasion was as unromantic as a recital by Clara Butt or a Liberal rally addressed by Sir Donald Maclean—no reflection upon Sir Donald who was one of my father's few intimate friends and a man of infinite kindness and honour.

We did suffer from our ignorance of art and music, but we suffered even more from our ignorance of all the more complex manifestations of Nature. We could study the flowers in the garden, the seashore, mountains and rivers, freely and without embarrassment, but not animals. It is often impossible to predict what movements a moving creature will make next, safer if prudish to ignore it altogether. Of our own bodies we were ashamed, and we were cut off from them, too, by the layers of thick and complicated clothing made necessary by the climate and poorly heated houses. I felt dismayed to observe in my bath that I had not been given even the fairly decent look of a furred or hairy beast, but was cursed with an ashen nakedness like something unfinished. If the early missionaries came from homes like ours, it was natural that they expended much thought and trouble upon dressing their converts. I remember my mother's scarlet indignation on Aberdeen beach when one happy little boy—only one among hundreds—was allowed by his parents to bathe without a suit. At that time my bathing suit had full bloomers that tied with a tape round my waist and a voluminous blue tunic almost down to my knees ornamented with rows of white braid. It was a wonder that I did not go to the bottom with the weight of wet material.

But when we did finally extricate ourselves from all these conventions and prejudices, it was very exhilarating. No one can hug liberty so close who has never been denied it. And then again, if I move the canvas just a little and let the light fall from another angle, our childhood seems hardly pitiable at all. We knew the Bible, a most untrammelled work, from our earliest days. We had Shakespeare and Milton and all the nineteenth-century novelists. Although the eye was neglected the ear for poetry never was. No one interfered with the growth of the senses of smell and touch, so deeply involved in the carnal pleasures of life, and the sense of taste had plenty of opportunity to become refined upon the simple but superb food of fifty years ago, the nutty-flavoured oats, the delicate home-made bread, the fresh butter and the traditional cheeses, fish caught within a stone's throw of one's home and brought to the door all-but alive by the fisherman's wife; snowy potatoes bursting from their unscarred skins; ruddy-yolked eggs of free-ranging hens;

new milk—not milk so treated that it keeps for days—
and home-grown fruit. It has become one of the main
tasks of the fastidious housewife to obtain these pleasures
which in my childhood were ordinary and universal.

Until I was nine, however, I was difficult about food
and scarcely appreciated any of these things, but fancied
mushrooms or coconut biscuits, which my mother spoilt
me by providing, giving the excuse that I ate so little else.
My brothers and sisters repeated these words at every
opportunity with proper scorn. But at nine I contracted
infective jaundice. It struck me suddenly and with great
violence and I vomited all through one miserable night.
When the doctor came next morning he put me on milk
and water for six days. This was drastic treatment. I
ceased to feel sick but turned as yellow as a guinea, even
to the whites of my eyes, and felt very weak. The in-
valid's bell stood by my bed, a brass bell with a handle
made of two Oriental figures standing back to back,
identical but for their faces. One had a low and sulky jaw,
the other looked quite agreeable. I brooded on their
sameness and their difference, being too weak to do much
else. When the aroma from the kitchen drifted up to my
bedroom, tears filled my eyes. My father read to me but
we found that every book in the house mentioned food
sooner or later, and my hunger made it quite intolerable
to hear of others eating. At last the six days came to an
end and I was propped up in bed and served a steamed
whiting, lying very naked and quite defenceless on a
plate. It had been skinned by the fishmonger and held its
tail in its mouth in the traditional fashion. I ate it flake by
snowy iridescent flake until nothing remained but the
skeleton. And from that day I was changed and fussed no
more about my food.

When my convalescence was complete and my health, though not my weight, normal again, I found that I was able to move about the house sometimes with the speed and agility of a lemur, enjoying that sensation of floating in the air that can make dreams so delightful. I used to arrange a few chairs or hassocks as stepping-stones, and put a girdle round the dining-room, scarcely resting even on my stepping-stones. I always avoided having a witness and even when I wished I did not always find myself able to 'fly', but I learnt to know by signs in myself when the hour was propitious. A year or so later this curious skill vanished as suddenly as it had come—call it Levitation if you will, or Lung Gom with the Tibetans— I had heard of neither. Almost at once I forgot about it and might never have remembered it again but that I read recently Mr Richard Church's *Over the Bridge*. Then as I came to his account of how he rose in the air at the convalescent home, and even floated downstairs without touching the treads, the memory of my own more modest experiences rose up in a flash from the past, so strange and unexpected a little ghost that my skin rippled to greet it.

The first winter at Aberdeen, two years before this illness, I went to Mr. Mackie's school, afterwards known as Albyn Place, and was wretchedly unhappy. I found none of the cosiness of the Miss Fishers' school in Berwick, no fun with scissors and coloured paper, no concessions to childhood. So my parents removed me for four years and sent me to the Girls' High School, promising Mr. Mackie that I should return to him as soon as I was old enough to benefit by his teaching of English, for which he was famous in the north. At the High School I passed into the care of Lucy Duffus, a member of my father's church, gay, pretty and full of vitality, and I must have given her a lot of trouble before I settled down. My mother took me as far as the Duffuses' house on the way to school in the morning and there I watched Miss Tibbie Duffus feed their large tom cat with morsels of fat bacon while Miss Lucy put on her coat and prepared to shepherd me to the school itself. Even after I grew to like school, starting off in the morning took a great deal of courage, and if at the last minute my pitying mother decided that I really had a nasty cold and kept me by the fire, I savoured with particular zest everything that made up home. The hours that chimed then from the black marble presentation clock on the mantelpiece, nine, ten, eleven, twelve, were not familiar at all, for in the general order of things I was at school from 9 a.m. to noon, and in bed from 9 p.m. to midnight. I sat alone in the warmth near the fire studying the face of the clock and feeling as if my mother had given me a wedge from the twenty-four hours that was still all fresh and unfingered. Such happiness could scarcely be adorned, and yet once it was adorned when Miss Bessie Lumsden (another kind member of the church) heard that I was at home with a cold and thought that I might need amusement. So she brought me a magazine to look at, and a pair of doll's scales, and a bag of chocolate pennies to weigh in the scales. This selection, so novel and imaginative, threw me into a trance of pleasure and gratitude. How could any mere human being, I wondered, know to choose so well, and I turned the pages of the magazine and weighed myself out a chocolate penny from time to time, through what seemed an eternity of delight, but cannot by the calendar have endured much more than one day.

There were boys as well as girls in my class at the High

School, and my first desk-mate was a boy in kilts. I could not bear the smell of cold skin which came from his knees and was glad to be moved presently to sit with a little girl in long black cashmere stockings like myself. The smartest and most interesting of all the little girls was Valerie Forrester-Thompson. A faint mauve glow came from beneath her smooth pale skin and her glossy hair was not plaited like mine or any ordinary child's, but coiled in some very cunning way and then caught with ribbons behind the ears. She had an air of great daring, and I found her very stylish, although I never knew her well for she was in a lower form and left the High School soon after I went there. She was one of the passengers killed on an airliner which crashed in Holland about 1930. When I read how she had jumped from the plane, not waiting with the other passengers for the crash, it was clear that she must always have lived up to the promise that she made at six.

Sir Herbert Grierson had been professor of English Literature and Language at the university for sixteen years when we first came to Aberdeen, yet it was only towards the end of my four years at the High School that I got to know his five daughters. I cannot believe that they had been there all the time, not noticed in the crowd, for they were like five cygnets in a pond of ducks and geese and moorhens; and I was not surprised that soon they all took flight—to Edinburgh in 1915. Mollie, Flora, Alys, Letty and Janet. Mollie was the loveliest of them all, with the complexion of a princess in a fairy tale. She trod the streets of Aberdeen and the corridors of the High School as lightly as if a poet had spread his dreams under her feet. Letty I knew best; she was big for her age and coltish, with a fringe over her wide clear eyes. She had inherited her mother's laugh, a great gusty warm laugh which years later resounded all over Woodlands wing at Girton from my room on the top floor and shocked Miss Hilda Murray down below. Letty astounded me now by saying that Bessie M—— (a mutual friend) was soft—she pronounced it almost to rhyme with daft —she brought all her boys up King's Gate to show them off to the Griersons. She implied that the Grierson girls had many greatly superior boys but would never deign to show them off and I expect that this was true. Very soon Professor Grierson was heard to say that if even one or two of his daughters could be stupid or unattractive, life would be much more restful. Until Letty made her comment on Bessie M—— it had never dawned on me that young women not in domestic service had the equivalent of followers, and although I now realized that this might happen in the best academic circles, I could not conceive that it would happen in our family.

I could read when I was six, but the great flaw of my reading books had been the over-illustration of the text, which rarely held anything that could not be guessed from the pictures. Most of my story-books had been so often read and recited to me before I came to tackle them myself that I scarcely knew whether my eye or my memory did the work, and I was over seven before I opened a book and had unpredicted thoughts and images conveyed to my mind by the symbols before me and by nothing else. It happened without warning, at bedtime on a summer evening, when the sunlight flickered through the plane trees and made a watery pattern on the wall of the big back bedroom. I picked up the pocket edition of *Alice in Wonderland* which my father had given to me a year before and began to read at the first para-

graph, which he had always skipped in reading aloud.
'Alice was beginning to get very tired of sitting by her
sister on the bank, and of having nothing to do. . . .'
This was bread-and-butter stuff to make my heart beat
so fast, but until that moment it had never occurred to me
that reading could mean finding out what one did not
know before, without asking anyone. By it all the secrets
of the world might be unlocked. More than that, it
seemed a sacrament and a miracle, my first intellectual
adventure and my greatest, the rapture of which was
never forgotten but touched every page of print from
that day onwards. At that moment I guessed nothing of
poetry. Poetry meant standing with my hands tidily
clasped behind my back reciting to grandparents and
aunts:

> *A fair little girl sat under a tree*
> *Sewing as long as her eyes could see.*

Rather than literature it was knowledge of a larger world
and the hope of explanation that excited me. Somewhere
the artist who drew the picture of the knight on horse-
back must have written down what he meant. In the
years between eight and sixteen I read with a persistence
and absorption and singleness of mind that never came
again. It was my greatest pleasure and at times my only
one. People I found tantalizing, disappointing, and also
very hard to please. They found me tense, opinionated
and smug. Games were tiring; lessons tedious. I never
finished the stories that I began to write, or found them
as good on paper as they seemed in my head. But reading
was always quite satisfying. When my mother drove me
out for fresh air and exercise, I read up a tree or sitting
hunched on the garden wall. Long after I was supposed

to be asleep I sat on the floor by my bedroom window, holding my book near to the bottom slat of the venetian blind, cautiously tilted to let through the last gleam of daylight. Not sent to bed, not driven into the garden, I took my book into the dining-room, tucked my legs under me on the little regency sofa, and ceased to be conscious of the actual world. I heard conversation so belatedly and with so little idea of its sense, that my parents and brothers and sisters would treat me as absent and beyond their reach until I had laid my book aside. These were the years of freedom from all responsibility and I made thorough use of them. I had no duties so laid upon my mind that I need ever feel that time was limited. My mother or my father would make sure that I went to school, that I ate my meals, that I did my homework and went to bed. Relaxed in the certainty of their unremitting watch, I could devote myself to a book with a thoroughness almost impossible for an adult. In addition to that, I had not learnt to criticize what I read. I was too eager to know anything to feel bored. Everything that came my way was news, life, food. Apart from the classical novels passed as suitable, *The Mill on the Floss*—but not *Adam Bede*, *Esmond*—but not *Vanity Fair*, I consumed a great deal of contemporary rubbish, school stories (of which the early Wodehouse in *The Captain* magazine were by far the best) and historical romances such as amuse hardly anyone today. Once my mother found me reading *The Prisoner of Zenda* (published by Nelson in a neat little edition which then cost sevenpence) on my unmade bed in the middle of a Saturday morning, and it was summer and the sun shining outside. This time she was very stern and sent me to play in the garden *without my book*. I went as far as the top step just outside the front door, and stood for a long time looking at the door and the hop vine climbing up the weather-worn freestone that surrounded it. I did not notice the sunshine, and my brother Archie would have said that a black dog was sitting on my back. To me it was something much worse. A choking, blinding cloud of discontent so filled and surrounded me that the difference between thought and feeling—clear and important at other times—was quite lost, and more appalling still, the powerful though miniature person-within-the-person who said 'No' or 'Yes' in the last issue and always had her way, she existed no longer. It was a new experience to feel so thoroughly disagreeable and I was frightened, like someone learning for the first time how bad a bad pain can be.

As everything on Sunday was different—clothes, food, behaviour—so was reading too, and we had a considerable stock of Sunday books. Many of these were little blue paper-covered volumes published by the S.P.C.K., melancholy stories dealing in extremes of poverty, depravity, misery and piety: *A Peep behind the Scenes*, *Froggy's Little Brother*, *Two Bright Shillings* and *Jessica's First Prayer*. We thought them much better stuff than the Sunday reading passed on from our parents, *The Fairchild Family* and *The Wide Wide World*. Their edition of *The Pilgrim's Progress* was complete, but ours—to show how the rot had already set in—had all the theological discussions left out (so it said on the title page) and over a hundred black and white illustrations. But the illustrators had done no expurgating and the picture of the body of Heedless, long dead, and the faces of the wicked ones who stepped up softly to Christian in the Valley of the Shadow of Death came very vividly to mind whenever one's temperature rose above normal. These pictures clothed and pinned down the primordial terrors which lurk in the minds of all children. Apart from *The Pilgrim's Progress* only one volume of our Sunday library survived to be read to the next generation, Jean Ingelow's beautiful, forgotten *Stories Told to a Child*, so delicate and true both in spirit and in its character-drawing.

In these days of story-reading I was still far too young to know the perturbation of any human lure, yet my heart jumped to attention at the first trace of a love story, no matter how simple and fragmentary. As surely as a gosling knows a blade of grass, I knew this as my staple need. Not in so many words, or in any words at all, but by moods of recognition, I acknowledged this to be the secret of all secrets, the deepest possible anguish and the highest possible bliss, as much of the spirit as of the body and perishing if not of both.

And yet many of my early memories link happiness with being alone. In a big family like ours, noise and a crowd was the normal state, at meals, in the nursery, in the little back garden at Berwick with its five small plots, or in the schoolroom at Aberdeen, afterwards called the Abomination of Desolation, spoken of by Daniel the Prophet. When all the older ones went off to school the quietness must have been sudden and striking, and perhaps it was then that I first observed that the silence was not always complete and that two or three people were talking together somewhere. When it proved to be neither grown-ups in another room, nor neighbours through the wall, I was puzzled, but in time resigned myself to hearing disembodied voices, assuming them to be my own invention although I had no control over them. There were other circumstances in which invention bolted from intention, for instance when I told myself stories in bed at night and was forced to accept the wrong kind of ending; and although I disliked hearing these voices, I don't remember being worried by the oddness of it. The tenor of this conversation would be clear enough, sometimes soothing and amiable, sometimes grumbling, and at other times quick and irate. I was obliged to believe that they discussed me and my doings, and even when they seemed in a good humour, I did not like this, and if I could break up the conversation I did, by singing at the top of my voice, running three times round the garden, or skipping on the pavement. But often I lacked the resolution to do this, and sat mesmerized over my cross-stitch, my drawing or my sums. I rarely heard them when I was reading a book, but certain quiet and repetitive activities I learnt to regard as dangerous: along those currents my thoughts might be sucked into a rhythm which proved to be also the rhythm of the voices. But what did they really say? My ears were never quite sharp enough to hear, and so it never occurred to me to compare them with the voices heard by Joan of Arc or Blake. As I grew up they became dim and infrequent; yet many years after they had ceased to trouble me I dreamt of underground passages all round the manse inhabited by troglodytes. The passages communicated with hollow places in the walls of the houses of Westfield Terrace, and in the dream I immediately thought: Why, that explains the voices. Later still, in the *New York Times* in 1941, the report of a paper read to the American Psychiatric Association on auditory hallucinations caught my eye—'found in a surprisingly large number of schizophrenia victims', it said. The speaker suggested that the echoes might be attributed to a feeling of external domination by some powerful agent—that I recognized at once, the viziers nodding together—or even a mechanical fault of the senses. He did not mention the sensitiveness shared by children and neurotics to inward movements, transitions in the blood, to growth and change. At night I used to complain that my tongue seemed abnormally large and that my fingers and toes had ceased to be part of my body. My mother might be inclined to believe this but my father gently assured me that I was imagining things and my tongue would not choke me, nor my fingers and toes refuse to do as I wished. The voices, on the other hand, I did not discuss with anyone—yet I am not sure that far, far back in childhood, I did not mention them, lightly, in passing, as a recognized evil, and thereupon see my parents look so startled that I took care never to speak of them again. How normal I assumed us all to be I can gauge by my astonishment in 1910 as I helped my father to fill in his paper for the census of the population taken in that year. There was a space in which to enter the number of children mentally abnormal, and as my father wrote 'None' he added to himself in a low voice, 'thank God'. I was abashed. I could not join in his thanksgiving until I had digested the amazing possibility that any of us could be otherwise than supremely sane.

Of all the moods and feelings that beset me the strangest was the briefest, lasting little more than the space between two heart-beats. I would wake in the grey light before dawn and know at once my room, my bed, the books beside me and everything but myself, which in that lucid moment hung far off like a little curtain in a very great space. Transfixed and stripped of all comfort and security, an 'I' that had no right to the title, yet asked with all the greater urgency 'Who am I?' and at once with that question life became normal again. But the impression remained that I had been within an ace of knowing the answer to the question. Now I should say that I was within an ace of knowing the question.

The normal alone seemed reliable. Something rigid in our notions made me neglect and even despise all unusual routes to knowledge. My ignorance of my ignorance in these deep matters was complete, encasing, impenetrable, like the shell round an egg. In ignorance itself there may be life and hope, but it must be acknowledged. I was taught that Sir Isaac Newton saw an apple fall to the ground in his orchard, and by putting two and two together—as was natural for a brilliant and original man—arrived at the Theory of Gravity. This dull little anecdote dried up my curiosity for a very long time, until I was privileged to read the papers given to the Royal Society at the Newton Tercentenary Celebrations, and discovered that Newton was a very peculiar man indeed, deriving his knowledge—as Professor Andrade said—'by something more like a direct contact with the unknown sources that surround us, with the world of mystery, than has been vouchsafed to any other man of science'. Then I saw too what Maynard Keynes thought of him: 'I fancy his pre-eminence is due to the muscles of intuition being the strongest and most enduring with which a man has ever been gifted.' Newton at a stroke became real. While his achievements were still far beyond my understanding, I could see a shape which might be the shape of the process by which he made his discoveries. Keynes had died before his paper on Newton was read to the Royal Society, so I have never been able to tell him of my gratitude. I would willingly have thrown out everything I was taught at school in exchange for that one sentence.

CHAPTER FIVE

Church

When we first went to Aberdeen, fields surrounded the cul-de-sac of Westfield Terrace on three sides. Behind the house lay the remains of the gardens of Ashley House, by that time running wild, and in front, the Dalgarnos' nursery gardens, and a rough steep hill leading down to the Den Burn, which at that point and others in the town flowed through a patch of meadow hedged with hawthorn bushes and wild roses. Nearer the centre of the town this stream appeared suddenly from beneath a culvert by some old houses, and on its farther bank were high trees where rooks built their nests. We took a passionate interest in these rooks. They reminded us children of Marshall Meadows and snowdrops, and my mother of Fort Etna. Their return each year signalled the end of another hard northern winter. We passed this tiny patch of old garden on our way to church and it consoled us a little for the ugliness of the rest of the walk. After that we plunged into Skene Street proper, in those days one of the many slum areas of Aberdeen. The houses built on the steep bank of the burn showed only one or two storeys on the side facing

93

the street and so appeared less forbidding than the high tenements of other quarters, yet a fearful greasy stench permeated the place, and loutish boys and girls fought and abused one another in the alleyways, using a language none of us understood, so harsh and turned with such strange phrases. This must have shocked my father with his strong Liberal views, and my mother with her tender heart, but their opinions and emotions at that time influenced mine very little. Skene Street offended sight, smell and hearing. I wished that we might go the roundabout way to church by Union Street, but even when all the shops were shut the atmosphere of Union Street remained so secular that this was out of the question. Very much later I began to wonder why I had been born into so much comfort and cleanliness, although a commoner question in those days was rather why not further up the social scale? My brother Jack, for instance, used to take many solitary walks as a boy in his teens, and when we asked him why he did so, he used to reply that he liked to think on life. This interested me greatly and I said: 'What do you think when you think about Life?' 'I wonder why I am not the Prince of Wales,' he answered promptly.

Unknown to us Skene Street was ripening in the dark to a little fame. Fifteen years before this time Frederick Rolfe (Baron Corvo) lodged in one of the taller houses. But he failed to pay his rent and was eventually thrown out in his pyjamas on the very pavement over which Sunday after Sunday we hurried to church, as light-footed as birds, never breaking through the thin crust of present things and the evidence of our senses.

An old-fashioned expression of my father's still sounds in my ears: 'Very humble people.' His congregation of eleven hundred or so members included some wealthy and cultured families, such as the Cooks and the Jaffreys and the Abernethys, also many with more culture than money, and some—the very humble people—who had little money, and by our severe Scottish standards, little culture. We were beginning to leave out the famous controversial stanza in the hymn 'All things bright and beautiful', yet any idea of a levelling of incomes such as actually happened before he died might have perturbed my father at that time. There was a sadder difference than that between rich and poor, the difference between believer and unbeliever, and the tendrils of our young thoughts were carefully looped round missionary ambitions rather than those of social reform. This choice was made clearer by the contrast between the unregenerate brawling poor of Skene Street and the mannerly poor who came Sunday after Sunday to sit under my father, people whose sharper needs were met from the church funds or by private gifts from wealthier members. Sometimes a very humble person showed an absence of spiritual humility, as the frail old woman whom we called the Dying Swan, who confided to a friend that she had great difficulty in understanding what the minister meant by Temptation. 'How are we timpted? I am niver timpted.' Near her in the front of the church sat our washer-woman, Betsy. (Seats in the church pews were rented, those right in the front being very inexpensive.) She was too deaf to hear the voices of the choir or the congregation and charmed us by the dogged way that she boomed on at her own pace through psalm and hymn and paraphrase until everyone sat down. It fascinated my brother Archie to try to discover just where the threshold of her remnant of hearing lay, so when she came on

Mondays to our cellar wash-house, he rolled an iron bucket down the stone stairs to the cellar until Betsy rushed out bellowing with astonishment. When she saw the bucket at the bottom of the stairs she used to give her deep chuckle and flap her hand as if brushing away a cloud of hornets, and say indulgently: 'It's-a Archie-a.'

At the time that we went to Aberdeen Miss Stephen must have been already well over eighty. She was a much honoured member of the church and lived near us in a tiny granite house packed with early Victorian furniture and relics of her family. It became quite a regular thing for me to call there on my way home from school and be presented with a peppermint cream by the maid Jannet. Miss Stephen herself was always sitting in the same chair on the right side of the fireplace in the front parlour, a little lean person in a long black silk dress which fitted closely at the tiny throat and the tiny waist. Her long ears, white and dead-looking, were dragged down by big gold ear-rings. She looked severe and her conversation consisted of questions, some of them distinctly inquisitive. I answered as well as I could for I held the old lady in great reverence. So did the gentle and good Jannet, ordered about by Miss Stephen as if she were still the little orphan girl who had come to her at eleven, and not a woman well past middle age. Once when I was gambolling past the house in a flurry of snow, Jannet called after me from the door, and I ran back with the snowflakes in my hair, to be given a stern message about the necessity of hats or bonnets in winter. After that my mother tied a scarf over my head in bad weather, not because she thought it necessary, but to please Miss Stephen. It was repeated to me, probably by my indiscreet mother who had it from my father, that Miss Stephen enjoyed my visits. What she liked particularly was my honesty. This unexpected and undeserved tribute had more effect than a hundred sermons. Great was the shame of being an ordinary fibbing little girl who yet passed herself off as particularly honest to such an old woman.

I am glad to say that Miss Stephen left Jannet very comfortably off. The mantle of this prophetess passed to her servant and became her very well. No longer a factotum but a lady in manner and dress, as she had always been in spirit, she was honoured by all and surrounded by friends. I believe that she earned and deserved more affection than her mistress ever had.

Although we hated the walk through Skene Street, none of us disliked church itself. There was a children's sermon, brief and tactful. My father never committed the *faux pas* so common with other preachers of bringing anecdotes of his own family into the children's sermon. The real sermon which followed was not as a rule too deep for a child to follow if the child was so disposed, and in any case the atmosphere of the manse pew itself was never dull. Our assembling in church crowned my mother's busy week. There were the six of us dressed in our best clothes, spotless and tidy with clean white fabric gloves and clean handkerchiefs, ranged three on either side of her in the order least likely to provoke struggles over hassocks or whispered recriminations about behaviour. My memory includes no unseemly scramble, but that may be because the responsibility lay so completely with my mother. Long after, Innes Logan, assistant to my father and charming friend to us all, wrote how well he remembered her 'sailing up the aisle in the South Church, large hat slightly to one side, arriving just in time, preceded and followed by her brood, until "some on rafts and some on broken pieces of the ship they all came safe at last to land".'

We had a good collection of Bibles permanently in the pew, English, German, French, Italian and Greek, with the delicate signatures of grandparents and great-aunts on the fly-leaves. Some of us also brought our own Bibles which held between the pages certain treasures, a sprig of verbena from Fort Etna, a skeleton leaf found in Rubislaw Den, a painted book-mark or even a little photograph; and poems and quotations of a spiritual nature might be written on the back of the map of Palestine, the plan of the Temple and the voyages of St. Paul. In following the Bible readings some fluttering of leaves was necessary before we found Hosea or Haggai, but we had no difficulty at all in finding our way among the books of the New Testament owing to a mnemonic which we mastered when very young.

> *Rum Cor Cor Gal Ephee*
> *Phil Col Thess Thessalee*
> *Timmy Timmy Tit Philemon*
> *Hebrews James Pet Pet John*
> *John John Jude Revelay-shy-on.*

While my mother taught us this rhyme and did not mind how quickly and frivolously we recited it, she objected very strongly to irreverent haste in such a matter as grace before meals. Our usual grace was 'Bless us O Lord and let our food strengthen us in Thy service, for Jesus Christ's sake. Amen.' She declared that we all ran the first four words into one 'Blessusolord' and made it a frantic demand rather than an earnest request.

My mother disliked the position of the pew, at right angles to most of the pews in the church and near the pulpit. Everyone could see us, and her upbringing had made her very sensitive to comment. At the same time she felt it her duty to see that nothing in our appearance should hinder the congregation from concentrating upon the service. The ostrich feathers that I remembered lovingly in her Berwick Sunday hats had passed out of fashion, but she wore creamy pink tea roses on her graceful wide-brimmed straws, and the milliner was always instructed to mount the roses on the left side, away from the congregation. When a new hat arrived one Saturday, too late to be returned, with all its roses on the side exposed to the congregation, my mother carefully shrouded them with a piece of black tulle.

To me the position of the pew seemed quite satisfactory. Without turning or appearing to stare (so I hoped), I could see many faces of wonderful authenticity. In the biting winds of Aberdeen men and women often looked middle-aged by thirty, but then, hard and healthy, they might change little for thirty more years, or forty or even fifty. This gave some of the older people a look of great strength and permanence. Their appearance by degrees became mosaics built into the walls of our young memories and part of the structure for the rest of our lives. And so we came Sunday after Sunday to the end of the service, always with a slight sense of relief, to the rousing words and tune of the paraphrase and my father raising his hands to pronounce the benediction. The reverence and meaning in his voice could not be ignored or misunderstood, the youngest stopped fidgeting and one and all we were indeed blessed.

The walk home from church, as soon as we had left Skene Street behind, turned into a pleasant stroll. We chattered together as cheerful as starlings and discussed the service with the interest and aptitude of connoisseurs. Once a vast cumulus cloud in the south-east seemed to follow us as the mountain peaks followed the boy Wordsworth. It was purple and edged with molten silver. I tugged at the sleeve of first one and then another brother or sister. Each followed my instructions and looked, but in such a cursory way that I appealed to my mother to command their attention. But alas, she looked not at the cloud but at me, saying with fond interest and pride: 'Yes, darling, I do see, it makes you feel excited.' I was too crushed to say anything more, but nothing could have brought home to me better the importance of tact in conversation and technique in art (which is largely a form of tact). If I wished to make others understand and share my pleasures, a method much more subtle than nudging and pointing and saying 'Oh look!' must be evolved.

Unlike going to church, going to Sunday School in the afternoon was always rather a trial to me. It was so soon to be returning down Skene Street, in winter leaving the good fire and the favourite melancholy books, or in summer the garden. The church hall was dark, its benches were hard and the hymns that we sang were dull and peculiar, out of flabby little dog-eared hymn books. Mr. George Cook as superintendent did everything that he could to counteract the unloveliness of Sunday School, by his proud bearing and his handsome ruddy face, his well-cut suits, his pleasant Scots accent and the frankness, even the ruthlessness of his utterances. His three wonderful daughters all took classes in the school, and while Anne, the youngest and smartest, taught my class, I felt slightly less unwilling to attend it. As a child, and even as I grew up, I was often surprised to hear people whom

I knew called handsome or beautiful or pretty when all I had realized myself was how I wanted to go on looking and looking at their faces, attributing my desire to some quality there which neither I nor anybody else could define. To learn that the quality was what the world knew as beauty came as a surprise not without its grain of disappointment. On the one hand it was gratifying to find that I had seen a handsome man or a beautiful woman, but on the other my pleasure was the less for being at last explained.

One day in the year we all went very gladly to the church hall, the day near Christmas when the church sale took place there, to raise money for the missionary we supported in China. Although called a sale, the name bazaar might have suited better. On the damask-covered stalls lay a great quantity and variety of merchandise, fine embroideries, needlework and knitting, carvings and paintings, dolls all furbelowed, hand-made toys of all kinds, shortbreads, jams and jellies. In addition the famous two-and-sixpenny lunch was served, cold chicken and ham and trifle (never too teetotal at that) and teas in which cakes and scones figured in a way that saddened us all for capacity to sample them fell so far below desire. On this superb day the noise in the church hall changed from the dry, restless chorus of Sunday school to a comfortable hum of kindly gossip and a resonant throb of Christian buying and selling. The smell of it changed from mothball and Lifebuoy soap to a fine yet strong spiciness, the smell of tea-cosies impregnated with hot, fresh tea, of plum cake and russia-leather purses. It was incense, yet quite Presbyterian and correct.

The sale was a festival, and so was Hallowe'en. It would have been as shocking to pass Christmas without celebration as the last day of October. We ducked for apples floating in a tin bath, or speared them with forks if the guests were afraid of germs. But were the apples Mr. George Cook's present, or some that my mother bought? Every autumn he sent us a huge barrel of Canadian apples, imported on one of his ships. They arrived in the dusk of an October or November afternoon by horse-drawn dray. The carter crunched heavily up our front drive with the barrel on his back and lowered it through the wide-open door on to the patterned tiles of the front hall: the brawny, grunting carter whose face I never noticed. Such figures become Pucks, touching the simplest events with emotion, our little moujiks, augurs of crisis. Forty years after this I camped alone in a deserted house, in the autumn again, and as the darkness came on heard an old man breaking up kindling-wood in an out-house, to give me a fire for company, and I felt the same stirring, the same flash of recognition which is never complete. Something cuts it short and a darkness heavy as soil covers the memory.

Mr. Cook's barrel was much too large for us to move. We unpacked it where it stood and carried the huge red juicy apples on trays and in baskets up to the attics for storing. Finally the barrel too went up to the attics for us to play with. For weeks it fumed of apples and we felt tipsy and faint if playing hide-and-seek we crouched in it too long. We were always playing hide-and-seek, Edward, Yda and I, either by ourselves or with a friend or two, and it was really not at all agreeable. The hiding holes were usually stuffy and uncomfortable and the hider so often forgotten or never found. To be apple-tipsy was not unpleasant, but the pungent, metallic smell from my mother's furs in her wardrobe choked me. I speak of hide-and-seek indoors. If we were allowed to play in the garden and the terrace in the dark, that was bliss, among the fallen leaves and under the stars. Then transported beyond all my normal ways of thought, I first felt myself not a child but a vessel shaped to receive all the gifts of the universe until filled and overflowing, until compelled to pour out what I had received as the ancient Hebrews poured oil upon their altars. Until death it remains the highest duty and the chief function, a summons without explanation, perhaps without justification, but impossible to ignore. It has linked me in sympathy, however little in performance, to the great ones of the earth. I think of the painter John Butler Yeats, the father of the poet, believing as an old man in exile that at last he was beginning to know how he wanted to paint, writing to his son: 'I am afraid you must sometimes think me very conceited—the fact is not only am I an old man in a hurry, but all my life I have fancied myself just on the verge of discovering the primum mobile.'[1] I think too of Beethoven on the triumphant production of the Ninth Symphony. A few years earlier he had nearly ended his life. 'My art however held me back. It seemed impossible to leave this world until I had produced all that lies within me.'

The goodness of the church folk at Aberdeen, their worthiness and strength of character, had so little charm for us as children that we pushed it from our thoughts, as something ordinary and uninteresting, when it was in fact both extraordinary and very interesting. But about my father's friend David Cairns, first professor and then principal at the Theological College, we all felt differ-

[1] J. B. Yeats, *Letters to His Son*, edited by Joseph Hone (Faber & Faber).

ently. Though modest as a person, he had a pride in his calling and in the tradition of the Church that warmed the imagination. The saints and martyrs took on flesh and blood as he spoke their names, and he followed the guidance of his own inner spirit with a fierce preoccupation. The Cairns family had belonged to our lives in Berwick when David Cairns was minister at Ayton just north of the Border. Mrs. Cairns called my mother Lilian and my mother loved her and called her Helen, and when they preceded us to Aberdeen by a year, it made the passage to the north easier for both my parents. A letter from my mother (still in Berwick) turned up among the Cairns papers recently, asking Mrs. Cairns for information on the two things of particular importance to her—the existence of a garden at the manse, and of a school in Aberdeen for the boys, run by Christian gentlemen.

Professor Cairns was a great shaggy man, very careless of his dress and appearance, with a brooding powerful face. His children collected stories of his absence of mind and used to tease and amuse him by asking him to correct or verify them. If a ticket collector came to his compartment on the train he would as like as not grasp the hand held out for his ticket and shake it warmly and pass the time of day, and then carry on his talk with his travelling companions. A few years after the tragically early death of his wife he called at our manse with a message for my father. My mother asked him to stay for tea but he excused himself saying: 'My wife will be expecting me at home.' My mother was heart-struck, imagining the fresh pang of bereavement when he stepped over his own threshold and remembered. Yet it may have been an even deeper forgetfulness in which the excuse from the past slipped back into the past as soon as he had made it.

When he did stay to tea his conversation was rich and original, full of varied knowledge, and so stimulating that my father himself glowed and talked as at no other time. In spite of these visits, and mine to play with his children, Alison and David, I never expected him to know me in the street. His deep eyes under their wild brows had the appearance of piercing through everything material to the truths and visions that absorb a prophet. But he always stopped. He would even cross the road if I walked on the other side. Then a little ritual was performed. He tapped my shoulder while I fidgeted a little and smiled self-consciously. His voice rumbled up from the deeps of his heavy ulster, his muffler, coat and waistcoat. 'Be virtuous', he said, 'and you will be happy.' Then he hurried on with an enigmatic gleam in his eyes. He knew that I did not believe it; he may even have doubted it himself, but at least the converse was true. Once, later on in Edinburgh, he discovered that neither Alison nor I had seen the tablet in Parliament Square which, carved with the initials I. K., marks the burial-place of John Knox. We had been in St. Giles' Cathedral; Professor Cairns was shocked at our ignorance and quoted in his deep rolling way, which never failed to thrill and move us, the words spoken by the Regent Morton over Knox's grave: 'Here lies one who neither feared nor flattered flesh.' We separated to hunt for the stone, and presently Alison and I saw that her father was standing devoutly with his black shovel hat against his breast and his venerable head bowed. Traffic and pedestrians circled away respectfully from this unusual sight, and we hurried with important faces to join him. Then we perceived that he was gazing down at the metal lid of a hydrant point, his face fixed in solemnity but his body shaking with amusement. In the same bold vein of humour when he lay dying he refused to be lifted for a little on to a rubber air-ring, branding it as 'a saddle most unsuitable for the transit from time to eternity'. He gave me the most valuable of all touchstones, for in him I learnt to recognize greatness, although without giving it a name. It was a long time before I could attach to him in my own mind a title given to such as Alexander and Pompey, Peter, Catherine and Frederick, famous names not particularly associated with freedom from vanity and personal ambition, or with charity and vision. So history and tradition confused my values for many years, but the lesson of a living character is indelible and in the end everything else goes down before it.

CHAPTER SIX

Holidays

I mentioned my father's diary in the first chapter and how he always recorded the direction of the wind. His interest in the sky and the clouds and the weather was consuming; he was an amateur meteorologist, and I regret that neither he nor anyone in the family thought of writing down the results of his observations and experience. The move to Aberdeen intensified this interest, for it was impossible for newcomers from the south not to become more sensitive to the seasons with their northern brilliance and violent changes—the summer so much lighter and the winter so much darker. Both winter and summer the heavy sea-haar rolled in without warning from the east, starting up the foghorn at Nigg, an unearthly moan rising to a bellow, like the call of a prehistoric monster (so we thought). My mother could not bear this foghorn, but I found something rather fine in the deep and powerful sound. From the slight elevation of the manse we could see over the town to the country south of the Dee where the first trace of the Grampians raised its non-committal head. On frosty mornings a flaming fur edged this quiet skyline. The orange melted into yellow, the yellow to green and the green to blue, a very hard Arctic blue against which the Morning Star pulsed with cold. Lagged from head to foot with immensely thick woollens, we just kept warm on such days. When the gales came, raging for three days and nights on end, even my mother agreed to shutting windows and even that did not keep out the wind, which knocked the venetian blinds to and fro against the window-sills and lifted the rugs on our bedroom floors. After this the spring seemed very sudden. A little bunch of us, Alison Cairns and the Forgan girls and I, went for a walk after school and found unbelievable coltsfoot and scylla in the wilderness round the derelict house where Byron had lived as a boy. My Hawick woollens seemed at the same moment intolerably oppressive. A deck-chair was sure to appear on the lawn at the bottom of our garden soon after this, for my father was quick to notice the change. He took no risks, all the same, and wrapped himself up completely in a steamer rug before sitting in it. He looked like a Red Indian, except that he sat with his knees crossed and held the manuscript of a sermon in his hand. The robins knew him well because he so often raked the drive to supply them with grubs and worms, and they used to make free of the toe of the suspended boot emerging from the steamer rug, by perching on it as they crossed from one side of the garden to the other.

A mild high sky with mackerel clouds and a gull flying seaward brought Balgownie beach and picnics again to our thoughts. We rarely went to the sands between the Dee and the Don, because other people went there too, but travelled to the deserted beaches to the north of Don mouth, a place that we grew to love more and more. During the salmon fishing season the fisher came down at high tide to the nets, and strode along the ropes from post to post to the deep water where the salmon, seeking to pass the line of flanking net, had entered the trap at the end. The fisher speared them in the trap and hauled them up in his net. I have never seen fish caught so on any other coast, and what seemed familiar and natural to me as a child, I remember now as a curious custom which I might have journeyed to watch in a foreign land.

The price for our cherished isolation at Balgownie came at the end of the day. After the walk from the beach to the Bridge of Don we had to catch one tram to the centre of the town and then change to another, laden as we were with spades and pails and baskets, bathing suits and towels. Then over-sunned and over-excited, in the warmth of a summer evening, we were often very restless in bed. My mother, tired herself, came up and turned our burning pillows and straightened our sheets; gave us drinks of water to cool our throats and Bible verses to settle our thoughts. Sometimes I thought that she spoke severely to Edward in his bedroom across the passage before she came to me and Yda, and then I said anxiously: 'You aren't cross with Edward, are you?' He often did the same on my behalf, although there was no collusion, and this amused and touched her. The greatest treat was permission to go to the window in our nightgowns, refreshing our feet on the cool boards, to gaze out upon the twilight green of the garden which in June became dark for no more than an hour or two. At the bottom of the front garden grew two lime trees, in their full summer foliage very heavy and soft and deep. I waited for a flounce of air to stir the leaves. Though it was seldom strong enough on such nights to reach my bedroom window, I hoped that it would throw the scent of the blossom to me, as even a little wave will throw a pebble far up the beach. The lime I considered a particularly English tree, sweet and enervating by comparison with the pine and the silver birch, and reeking of Tennyson and Matthew Arnold.

Occasionally we went inland and picnicked by the Dee. I remember trying to fill the kettle from the river, but at every dip I brought up a score of tiny eels. Then we looked closely and saw that the whole river was seamed with young eels heading upstream. All the afternoon we watched, dipping in our cups and returning the inevitable catch. They were as countless and continuous as the flakes of snow in the great snowfall of our first winter in Aberdeen. I did not know until I sat under Sir J. Arthur Thomson many years later at Marischal College that I had seen the famous procession of eels, and that these little creatures had been hatched in the Gulf of Mexico and were merely a trifling remnant of the army that had crammed the Gulf Stream at the outset of their miraculous journey back to the streams and pools where their ancestors had spent their adolescence. Suffering and death preyed on our minds a good deal, and we liked to remember that no sparrow died without God to comfort it. But was there a line beyond which divine love could not step? Were the eels with the sparrows, or was the sparrow of more value than many eels?

Even before we moved to Aberdeen our holidays had often been spent in Scotland, at Ettrick Bridge End in 1904, Ballinluig (in the stationmaster's house) in 1905, and Crawford in 1906 and 1907. Ettrick remained in my memory for a lean-to, a brother on its tiles and a dog barking in the yard below. My mother said that I ran round the house from the shade and flung out my hands to the hot bright sun, crying: 'I can feel Jesus.' She saved

this as a proof of my early faith, but it must have been a
simple physical delight for which I snatched the name of
Christ as the only superlative yet in my vocabulary.
Whereas the gaps in memory from three or four onwards are like the fading away of life caused by natural
sleep, the blank periods before the age of three are more
like unconsciousness under an anaesthetic when even the
knowledge of a gap is blotted out. There remains a flash
of lightning, the lamp on the kitchen table, a barking
terrier, my hand going out to take a piece of madeira
cake (while someone assures me I am three years old), but
in between nothing at all. Of our Ballinluig holiday in
1905, so quickly does apprehension cohere after three
years of age, I remember a great deal: playing with
bundles of firewood with the stationmaster's daughter,
enjoying my clean white pinafores with frilled yokes, and
a hot dramatic day when we went to pick wild rasp-
berries and Edward disturbed a nest of wasps. He was in
a wood, on the wrong side of a barbed-wire fence from
my mother, who lifted him over in such haste that she
scored his bare legs on the barbs. We hurried to a cottage
for blue-bags and lint. Two young school teachers were
staying there and one went indoors to help my mother
with Edward while the other held the baby Yda and hor-
rified me by offering her a slice of plum cake. Then my
mother came out of the cottage and explained that I was
quite right, baby did not eat plum cake. (Baby would
have loved it.)

Among my Aunt Helen's papers was a letter from
Aunt Christina marked 'Keep for future gen.' by Aunt
Helen. It is headed simply 'Ballinluig. Tuesday' and I do
not think that the writer had any thought of future gens
at the time.

'We have had a truly glorious day to-day, which was most fortunate as we had a garden party of 20 altogether. All the Johns and the whole party from Moulin. To-morrow all the nursery party and John and Lilian are going to spend the day with them, with the exception of Baby who will stay with me. At present the children have such an excellent reputation among the Great Aunts it is quite painful trying to keep it up. So far all has gone well except behind the scenes occasionally, & today Lilian seems more rested and therefore happier and less nervy. Up till now she has been "patient" which is the most odious virtue on earth. I am glad you are taking A. & E. back with you for a short visit, it will be a real help to Lilian. 6 children and one servant are a handful. We have some truly funny scenes at times. Elsa in the sulks retires to a distant part of a field to sit alone. Suddenly there is a yell of "Help Help I've sat on an ant heap." Lilian and I just lay and cried with laughter. Lyn Lloyd sheltering under a bridge from icy wind and rain, growing more and more silent. Edward with a waterproof over his head sobbing as he tried to pull his boots over cold feet covered with wet mud. All having been allowed to fish for minnows, wading on a day that we ought to have had a fire! Elsa perched on a high pole (all trying to find a dry spot under the bridge) suddenly poked by Archie falls prone within two inches of a roaring torrent into mud and wet. Baby won't stay in go-cart; will prance round. No cloaks, no hats, Jack sits apart and looks on with a quiet smile. Rain continues to pour in torrents. Lyn Lloyd suddenly breaks her most gloomy silence with a stolid sort of shout: "I WANT A MUFF." It was so funny if you could only have seen it all. At last we made a desperate rush for home and arrived soaked. We dried them all and warmed poor little Lyn's cold hands and vowed never to go minnow fishing again on a cold day with pouring rain ready to come down any moment.'

As Christina never married and Helen though married had no children, both these aunts had more time than is usual for nephews and nieces, and no branch of the family was larger or more in need of their help than ours. Later on Christina became principal of a missionary training college at Selly Oak, and made her mark in the world, but until she had her students, we were a little over-aunted at times. My mother never felt quite at ease with Christina and her forcible character over-shadowed Helen's, who was in her quiet way the more original of the two. With less reputation to keep up, she found it easier to be frank about herself. We observed that her anecdotes of childhood pointed fewer morals than Aunt Christina's. Aunt Helen and Uncle Thorburn, young things dreading the journey from Liverpool to Glasgow, by reason of their unreliable stomachs, wrote for a box of tracts advertised as issued free for distribution. They found, as they hoped, that in giving away these tracts, their thoughts were agreeably distracted, but unfortunately when they left Carlisle there were still hundreds of tracts left in the box and the individual approach became impossible. They were obliged to pitch them out of the window in handfuls at every station, or even to groups of workmen on the line. In Christina's hands this story would have stopped at the Border, but Helen had been born with a desire to preserve the truth, however unconventional, sad or shocking (Mamma dying, Papa groaning at the dinner table). Without any ambition to write, she had a passion for keeping records, and through her the gulf between the attitude of each of my parents was spanned for me. She made a sense of history (my father's talent) into a more genial and human thing by taking as her subject each day as it passed, and the material of such traditional family *contes* as my mother knew and loved she gathered in carefully with the rest. Everything was grist and her mill tireless and methodical. Many facts too personal to appeal to my father and far too humdrum for my mother seemed to her to be worthy of preservation. She kept letters, cuttings, relics, tokens, photographs, diaries, commonplace books. A few of these she marked 'for future gens.' but in the main she was guided by a spirit of blind but persistent research. Life, moment by moment, was real and delicious to her, she could not bear it to vanish unrecorded. In an old and empty needle-case which had found its way into my workbox I noticed recently a tiny piece of folded paper, and when I unfolded it I read this in Aunt Helen's handwriting: 'Musselburgh fishwives wear 15 petticoats $4\frac{1}{2}$ yards in each the flannel 2/6 a yard.' That was very interesting to me. No wonder that Great-uncle Scott in Musselburgh thought me insufficiently clad, a wisp of a child in one flannel pettitcoat and a white serge skirt.

At one time we were rather amused by Aunt Helen and thought her more of an old maid (in spite of Uncle Norman) than Aunt Christina herself. When she relined the exquisitely tidy drawers of her hautboy, she noted the date of the relining on the corner of each sheet of white paper. We marvelled at the finicking care with which she planned holidays abroad. She never left for a foreign country without buying a stock of gospels in the appropriate language, and these she distributed quite differently from the tracts in the train, in whimsical and ingenious ways, hiding them on the top of wardrobes or down the sides of sofas, in the expectation that astonishment would lead the finder to study the good work more earnestly. Her motto 'It's all for the best' annoyed us. We laughed at our mother's favourite: 'When one door shuts, another door opens,' but at least it showed a fighting spirit, while Aunt Helen clapped her old-fashioned plaster on every sore place and made an end of it. Until we saw the stoicism and faith behind her commonplace words, the temptation to scoff overcame us. In reality both these aunts were women of indomitable spirit. Christina, acutely ill, alone but for a nurse hurriedly engaged by the doctor, the very day before she died found the nurse incompetent and gave her notice.

Aunt Helen must have been the prettier of the two when they were both young. She looks quite lovely in the old photograph, her elbows on a fur rug thrown over the back of a chair, in a velvet dress with a fine lace collar. But when she began to invite us and the Willie cousins to her big Glasgow house she was in her middle thirties, then a sober age, and growing matronly in figure and dress. She would have considered powder or lipstick most unladylike aids to her appearance, and she was marred a little by lines on her smooth forehead, pince-nez on her pretty nose, and a sadness about her mouth. She was disappointed to have no children of her own. But she was excessively fond of animals and kept besides her small dog, a large cat which used to hunt the neighbours' Darwin tulips and carry his gorgeous prey home to Aunt Helen in very good condition. From her I learnt how to speak to cats. We thought her very lucky to be married to Uncle Norman with his jokes and his roguery and comic ballads after his day's work was done. The work itself—the doctoring of thousands of worthy Glaswegians—he performed with an unruffled competence and suavity which impressed me deeply. His consulting room had the atmosphere and richness of a holy of holies and made the idea of being a patient most romantic, hardly connected at all with pains and aches, and a thousand miles from anything like death. It was altogether thrilling to stay with Aunt Helen and particularly to wake up each morning in the high and chilly spare room with wistaria-patterned wallpaper. Outside lay the grey streets, and the sound of many sirens called the workers to their factories, strange sounds that I could almost see, sprouting like fungus from among the chimneys.

CHAPTER SEVEN

The Snow Patch

Our first summer at Aberdeen we went to Cullen on the Moray Firth, and there Jack was nearly drowned, swimming beyond his depth on a strong ebb tide. Archie was with him and battled to the shore to tell my father who reached Jack just in time, but was hampered bringing him in because the boy did not know how to float on his back. After that we were all taught how to float on our backs as well as to swim, and learned to look upon the sea as a cunning and treacherous acquaintance. It gave us so much pleasure, but we could never be quite sure of our lives with it. My father coached us in tides and currents, sand-banks and water-holes and quick-sands, and never allowed us to bathe when we were very hot—or very cold—or immediately after a meal, in case we should be seized with cramp. Then he decided that eleven months by the sea every year was enough for our health and his nerves, and all our summer holidays after the one at Cullen were spent among the hills, usually on Speyside.

The first of these was flawless. We had rooms in a farm-house a mile or more from the river at Boat-of-Garten, among the pinewoods and the moorland on the hillside. The farm people gave up most of the low white house to us and crowded into sheds and farm-buildings at the back, pushing the animals out into the fields. Even for us it was very simple. The water was pumped up from a well in the yard and Yda fouled the pump by putting down some pebbles which she hoped to see shoot back again when she jerked the handle. The sons of the house were very angry to find the pump out of order and suspected that one of the boys had done it from mischief, but when they knew it was Yda their anger melted at once, for Yda wove circles round everyone. When the holiday came to an end they offered her a calf as the best thing that they had to give, but we could not think how to keep a calf in the garden of the manse, so the present was refused. It was shortly after this that in family conclave over making ends meet, I did suggest keeping hens in the back garden, and was told that the crowing of the cock would disturb us and all our neighbours. 'Hens will lay eggs. You don't need a cock.' This was taken as an example of my childish ignorance of sex and greeted with patronizing laughter. I blushed all over. I knew what they thought, yet I was sure that I was right, but with three brothers and a sister and even my mother against me, I could not argue the point.

The reasons for my parents' standoffish attitude to animals were plain enough. They had stocked the manse with enough young life already. Pets cost money to keep —even canary seed for my Dicky was an item—and they might be noisy, were almost sure to smell or cause smells to be. Also at that time there existed very generally a belief that dogs must be beaten, and if you disliked violence, as my parents did, you avoided keeping a dog.

Since the trainers of dogs—unlike the trainers of boys—have changed their views and methods, dogs have improved greatly. In my childhood they fought often with terrifying ferocity, and put the fear of death upon all cats, whereas now the shoe is upon the other foot. Moreover, neither dogs nor cats understood about gardens but buried bones (or something worse) right in the middle of the seedlings; and dogs had a particularly irritating habit of wiping their feet on the lawn. We were often scolded for not shutting the front gate carefully. When we forgot all the dogs in creation came in, so my mother declared.

In some ways my mother would have welcomed a cat in the house, to give us pleasure and keep the mice within bounds, although the *mawsy* warmth of a cat upon her knee was something she detested. But she had no skill with them, no idea how to train them or feed them or nurse them or talk to them, so after some tragedies we gave up trying. As it was rather a puzzle to her why God had dressed up men and women in bodies the way He had, one could hardly expect her to be reconciled to beasts which appeared to live almost entirely to eat and reproduce.

But flowers. She considered the lilies of the field with rapture: for their scent and colour, shape and texture, for their ignorance not only of toiling and spinning but of cooking and bearing children. They took nourishment so simply from the sun, the earth, the dew and the rain, and yet knew no problem of digestion or elimination. And their sex life seemed perfect to her, entirely by proxy. We were never allowed to burn dead flowers or put them in a dustbin, and I do it now only with a shudder. They were laid with leaves and other dead flowers in a special open grave-yard in a shady place in a corner of the back garden. But roses died rather soon in my mother's care. She loved the smell and feeling of them too much and could not forbear to bury her nose in them again and again. We used to find them tucked back in the vases to drink, but past all hope of recovery, her ravished victims.

But my grandfather in Birkenhead felt differently about animals, and saw how much they give to man and how great his duty in return. As a key thrown over a high wall, he sent me a magazine called *The Animal World* which may have been the source of my information about hens and eggs.

But to return to Boat-of-Garten in 1909: I can think of no emotional or physical crisis which should make that summer especially happy, yet it remains more of a whole and brighter and clearer than any other period of my childhood. We had a very quiet sort of time. The older boys walked or climbed or played golf with my father, and Elsa went with them whenever she could, for she hated being less free and active than a boy. But Yda and I and sometimes Edward usually stayed with my mother around the farm. I had a little white ninon scarf which I loved to wave as I danced and ran, but it frightened the geese and they chased me into a barn. I stood behind the door almost fainting with terror and breathlessness, until I noticed a round hole in the top of the door. I climbed up and boldly waved my scarf through the hole, which alarmed the geese so much that my mother pronounced it cruel.

In the afternoons Yda slept and I rested on my bed. The yellow calico blinds were drawn down and the blue-bottles hit them in their mad career. I thought that the bluebottle made a pleasant twanging noise, a song of summer. We used to get up very early in the morning, partly owing to Aunt Christina who was staying with us, fresh from a tour of India and accustomed to tea and thin bread and butter at six o'clock. She drank her tea out of doors, sitting in the sun on a little bench in the front garden of the farm—a simple little garden consisting of a narrow flower-bed under the windows, a pebbled path, and then the mountain grass scythed short for a space, and wired to keep the cattle out. The mist lay on the Spey like a soft smooth bolster. Sometimes it drifted up over the dark green of the Abernethy Forest which covered the lower slopes of the Cairngorms on the far side of the valley. We ate little pieces of Aunt Christina's bread and butter from her plate and watched the sun draw the mist up from the river.

A little to the left of the house just at the edge of the garden stood a small stone house all by itself. It may have been a dove house, but it was quite empty, clean and cool. I went down two or three steps into the single room and marvelled that anywhere could be so empty and clean and quiet. Two or three large snails meditated on the walls, their backs furrowed like bark. Farther off from the farm lay pine woods full of ant-hills, where Edward and I hunted for many hours for the crock of gold, left according to local legend by a careless miser behind a tree which he forgot to mark. While hunting for the gold I became persuaded that a very small breed of fairy might live in these woods. The toadstools grew in sociable groups, often a large one for a table, dimpled and holding dew in the dimples, with smaller toadstools growing round it for seats. I amused myself provisioning the feasts, with rowan berries for apples, harebells for goblets. Under larger toadstools, sometimes curtained with grass, I laid sprigs of bedstraw, and thought when I returned a day or two later that the beds had a used look. Aunt Christina read aloud the *Sky Pilot* by Ralph Connor on the lawn after dinner each day. This had nothing at all to do with flying. Hardly anyone had seen an aeroplane in those days. It was a western story with a religious message and a very watery love theme. We thought it absorbing, and I was scolded by everyone for daring to sneak away with the book and read on by myself.

We never returned to Boat-of-Garten, though we saw it from the train sometimes on our way to Newtonmore, where we spent July for many years. The scenery at Newtonmore was more rugged and the kind of place where we liked to picnic more accessible. My father used to rent one of the little villas recently built by the inhabitants in order to make a few pounds out of townsfolk in the summer months. Each summer we went to a different house, but they were much alike, furnished very cheaply, not at all with the unvarnished dignity of a backwoods shack, but in shoddy imitation of middle-class elegance. On each mantelpiece stood two specimens of the kind of crockery still to be won in shooting ranges at country fairs, and in each empty grate the owners had unfurled a confection of coloured tissue paper. Its smell, stuffy and old fashioned, came to be closely connected with Highland holidays. Even here man showed little of the good taste of his Creator. Beauty was the rule outside, but ugliness inside, and the smell of tissue paper a poor effort in comparison with the smell of bog myrtle.

The Cairngorms lay ten miles or so east of Newtonmore, rising in a blue wall from Glen Feshie. I gazed at the violent cleft made in this wall by one of the tributaries of the Feshie—the Allt Ruadh, I think—imagining it to be the entrance to the Larig Pass through which ran a rough and arduous footpath to the Linn of Dee. A friend of Elsa's had set out to do this long walk in ordinary shoes, and all but fell by the way. I watched the clouds descend upon the summits of the Cairngorms and hang a level canopy over the gorges. The next morning everything was lost in the rain which fell for two or even three days without ceasing. When the sun returned we could see a silver weal scoring the great wall of the mountains, a rope of water let down from the plateau to the Feshie two thousand feet below.

Now I began to play golf on a golf course, very badly and without any pleasure in the game, but under the impression that golf is an inevitable part of life. I usually went round by myself after the serious players were out of sight, and once as I was returning to the golf house, a village boy passed me, gasping horribly as he ran up the slope. He held one hand with the other and a scarlet handkerchief wrapped round his wrist. Some men gathered round him excitedly at the golf house, and I realized that the handkerchief had been scarlet with blood. He had overbalanced in the back of the cart which took the rubbish to the tip near the river, and fallen on a broken bottle, severing the artery in his wrist. I did not share Aunt Helen's love of accidents. 'I don't want them to happen,' she used to say, 'but if they must happen, I should like to be there.' One day as I was returning from school in Aberdeen a butcher's van went up Albyn Place at a spanking pace—butchers always had the fastest horses and milkmen the slowest. The butcher's boy dashed out of one of the houses where he had run ahead with an order while the driver served another client. He had done it scores of times, caught a rail and sprung into his seat beside the driver. This time he fell, and the wheel of the cart went over his legs. He looked straight ahead with an expression of great astonishment, turned coppery-red in the face, let out a bellow, and then flopped back on to the pavement. All this happened in a couple of seconds, and I waited for no more. The boy at Newtonmore recovered from his cut but I never knew what happened to the butcher's boy. I hated such things because they wore deep tracks in my memory, and I found my thoughts sliding that way too often and too easily.

I think that I may have found the boy with the scarlet handkerchief a welcome excuse for playing less golf, for my later memories of Newtonmore are mainly of walking on the moors and hills and bathing in pools in the Calder. A young cousin of our name was asked when he went to Eton if he were related to three fair-haired girls who used to walk by themselves over the moors of Speyside, who were known to this master and his companions as the Three Graces. This surprised us very much, not merely to be admired, but to think that anyone had observed us. We on our part never saw any masters from Eton.

Our wonderful holidays taxed both our parents in various ways. The rent of the house was about £15 for the month, a great deal of money for my father to find. Usually our maid came with us, so that meant nine tickets to buy. My father loved railway travelling and all the lore connected with it. He knew his time-table almost as well as he knew his Bible. But all this familiarity never made him a happy-go-lucky traveller, and he arrived at the station a good half-hour before the train was due to leave, although he had purchased the tickets the day before. In his pocket was a neat list of our many pieces of baggage, and this he checked perpetually. The actual packing and deciding what to take for the eight of the family fell largely to my mother and I cannot imagine how she got to bed at all the night before we left. I remember my father standing in the hall making up his list while the cabs approached. The house seethes with children in stages of preparation, the older ones arguing and excited, the younger already beginning to feel the motion of the train. My mother calls down the stairs: 'John, John, please strap up the Chinese basket.' My father's voice a minute or two later replies, somewhat tight and grim: 'It's impossible, my dearest, you have *packed in the lid*.' And although the two halves of the Chinese basket looked enough alike to make my mother's mistake most natural, we discovered then that the lid held a great deal more than the under half. My mother's last item is a shopping basket with sandwiches and fruit, reading matter, knitting, a ball and finally a kitchen cup with an envelope pulled over it. Archie looks in the cup and finds it half full of cold porridge left over from breakfast, whereupon we all side with my father and say it is the last straw and cannot be allowed.

But it was by saving the cups of cold porridge and similar economies that my mother brought many of the amenities of our childhood within reach. Because she never wasted anything her tiny housekeeping allowance stretched to birthday presents, hair-ribbons, spades and pails, pencils and rubbers, and such yearly treats as going down to the Aberdeen Dairy and asking for a sixpenny strawberry ice and three saucers and three spoons—for me and Edward and Yda. Her very remarkable talent for cooking was always challenged by poverty. Her soups were famous—made of prayers, so she claimed. Uncle Walter arrived at Berwick manse unexpectedly, late on a Sunday evening, and talked for years afterwards of the exquisite nameless dish that she provided. In fact when he appeared my mother had gone to the kitchen in some dismay, knowing that there was nothing in the larder but potatoes and half a cold kipper.

Probably on the eve of our summer holiday the scrapings of the porridge pot were even more carefully watched because she had to go away without paying the last grocer's bill. We knew that this happened in a round-about way. My father had rather a strong singing voice, not unpleasant from the pulpit but too loud for my mother's sensitive eardrums when he sat next her in church on holiday. She complained of this to him on the way home from church and said that she had even been obliged to tear pieces off the unpaid bills in her pockets in order to stuff her ears. My father may have been sympathetic but he laughed quite immoderately.

Soup, I ought to say, was not the only thing that my mother made with prayers. She resorted to prayer at every turn of the way, not because everything else had failed but before other solutions had time to fail. Those odd corners of time, going to post a letter, changing one's shoes, waiting to be served in a shop, that some fill with day-dreams, others by mulling over the past, my mother stuffed with prayers—always expecting an answer, usually in the form of a miracle. At least enough miracles were granted to satisfy her, but not enough to make her blasé. She was not surprised when they happened and did not grieve when they were postponed. When we grew up and scattered over the world her prayers followed us bringing unmerited boons and spectacular deliverance from evil all bearing the familiar hall-mark. Mother has been at it again, we wrote to one another, and although truly and humbly grateful, we were also a little scandalized, as most Christians are when anyone takes the Sermon on the Mount literally. She also prayed eagerly and tenderly for many hundreds of people she had never seen and could never expect to see, and flung a net which caught up many to whom prayer was an unfamiliar and inexplicable transaction. Of my friends Hermann and Hella Weyl (whose memory shines perpetually for all who were so happy as to know them) she had heard only through letters from me, and they knew her only through what I had told them. But once in hospital in America, with Hella two thousand miles to the west and my mother three thousand to the east, I received a little packet from Hella containing a silver and turquoise cross with a card to say that it was just to remind me that my mother was praying for me.

We made our last visit to Newtonmore during the war, when all the family had scattered in war service except my parents and me and Yda. Our maid, Helen Marshall, an intelligent and spirited young woman, came with us on a picnic that I remember particularly well. We had tea on the moor to the north of the valley, by a favourite burn, a tributary of the Calder, and when the time came to go home the sunlight was so bright and the air so clear that a patch of snow on one of the mountains of the Monadhliaths seemed no distance away. It was rare for us to see snow on anything lower or nearer than the Cairngorms, and we had watched the patch, very slowly shrinking ever since we arrived at the beginning of the month. This particular evening the attraction was too strong and Helen and I decided to walk to the snow while my parents and Yda went home. But the light and the clearness of the air had deceived us and we were soon beyond our usual range, committed to a long walk and a stiff climb. The snow was not on the first hill. We descended into a glen and started up the second and higher hill, now far further from home than we ever intended to be and with the sun setting. The beauty and the loneliness of the place laid a spell upon us. There was no wind at all and when we stopped for a moment to rest, we could hear a bee, like us benighted, seeking its home in the heather far down below. To turn back before getting to the snow became as unthinkable as turning away from love or truth. We did not even discuss coming again another day because we were both sure that such a day would never come again. Although the sun sets very late in Inverness-shire in July, it had gone when we reached the snow at last, no mere patch, but a little field of snow, and not pure white as it seemed from the village, but ribbed with brown deposit. Helen scooped a little of it into a handkerchief as a pilgrim might fill a bottle with water at a holy well, and then we started down. I was already very tired, and it was not even all down hill. But for the long twilight we could never have found our way at all. On the moor a mile or so from the village my father met us stumbling along. He had been patrolling there anxiously ever since sunset. He blamed Helen for letting me go so far; she answered him pertly and I felt sorry and ashamed that she could do such a thing. I paid for the pride that had kept me on my feet for the last two hours with a night of fever and pain, and a muscular weakness not to be cured for thirty years. One of the rules of our childhood was 'Stick it out.' 'Don't give in,' we urged one another, and 'Never say

Die.' (Rather die than say it.) Fusses and scenes in public were completely taboo. It had never occurred to me that I might lie down on the hillside and wait for two strong men with a stretcher to bring me home. And even years later in very tight corners, possibly with a child on my arm and luggage far too heavy to lift, the idea of sitting down on the platform or in the street until aid came never entered my head. But now I know, and act upon the knowledge, that it pays to give in. Policemen are professional Good Samaritans, so are firemen and even members of the forces. And ordinary people everywhere—those who have kept their simplicity by supplying the basic needs of other men—come easily and naturally to the rescue.

As a rule our Highland picnics came to an end long before sunset, and we ate supper at home and retired to bed with a book before it was dark. From the window of my bedroom I could sometimes pick out the very place where I had been, now looking as if no human foot had ever trodden there, with the rain perhaps and the cold mists sweeping across it. Difficult then to reconcile all the thoughts and sensations that this sight aroused. Delicious satisfaction with shelter and warmth pitted itself against longing to return at once and know the beloved place at an hour and in weather belonging—so it seemed—to its truest nature. While I knew very well that I stood by the bedroom window, and not out there on the hillside, I wondered how I could be so certain, with only the trifling ingredient of a little time to make so great a difference. For it was a great difference and there were insuperable barriers in the way of my returning. My father and mother would have thought me mad to suggest it, and my own strength and courage were unequal to such an undertaking. And that was not all, though the rest could not be put into words. Not-me, not-there, not-now, three interlacing themes of great charm. I liked to stand leaning and balancing on the wooden fence at the top of the railway embankment watching the rare train go through carrying poor people home whose holiday had already come to an end. Then somehow the disaster of the last day overtook us too, and we were no longer the favoured, but in a train ourselves. As we flashed out of one cutting into another, however, I caught a glimpse of someone leaning and balancing on the fence and felt almost sure that she wore a blue djibbah and a white blouse over which her hair fell in two long pigtails, and even that her birthday was on May 3rd.

CHAPTER EIGHT

The Human World

Wloved our picnics and walks and our holidays
among the mountains all the more for the late-
ness and difficulty with which we found our
places in a human world. In Nature we found solace
for understanding the world so little, and yet perhaps
Nature itself was to blame, and drew us apart. The
Human World—a magazine on that subject, handled in
the same simple and informative way as the matter of the
Animal World, would have been very acceptable. Late
at night in the block of tenements at the bottom of
Craigie Loanings, a couple of hundred yards from the
manse, an accordion wheezed into a kind of melody and
the tipsy, raucous voices of men and women joined in.
And from the same place there often came a terrible
sound of children crying. Both the sorrow and the
revelry were entirely beyond my reach and I was gripped
with a feeling of estrangement and frustration from
which I could see no escape.

My father was a convinced and strict teetotaller—not
so his father or even my mother for that matter—but
what taught us distrust of wine and spirits was the com-

mon sight of men the worse for drink, as they said, an expression of kindly implication. Sometimes a reveller was sleeping off his whisky in the gutter of Skene Street on a Sunday morning, and Archie saw a drunk man roll from the top of steps near the station the height of a house, and pick himself up at the bottom and stagger away. Another drunk tried to batter his way into our house late at night, roaring very loud. It was as bad as a grizzly bear drumming for entrance, and my father who had risked his life to save Jack in the Moray Firth, who visited regularly in the Fever Hospital (the very name of which terrified most people) was sadly non-plussed. I remembered this long afterwards when a Russian woman who had escaped during the Revolution said to me: 'It is terrible to be in a wood with a wild animal, specially if the wild animal is a man.'

The daughter of Mr. Dalgarno, the nursery gardener across the road, was attacked by a couple of rough strangers one night, on the hill that ran down from our house past their ground. We heard her calling her father loudly and persistently and after a long time—so it seemed to me listening apprehensively in bed—he came to her rescue and drove them off and helped her half-fainting into the house. Even before this happened the idea that an 'undesirable character' (always quite different from a very humble person, or as the Cairns family said: 'very plain people'), might be lurking in the bushes, had cut short our favourite games of hide-and-seek on autumn evenings. Then during the war when all the undesirable characters, poor fellows, were in the trenches, there came a lull in parental fears, and I might dance on the lawn at night if I wished. If it came over me—as the desire to play the piano came over my mother—then I danced and danced, not a polka nor a reel, but the wild natural steps of a wingless creature longing to fly, particularly when the moon was full and the wind blowing mildly: exquisite pleasure, as leaping and turning, running and skipping, I waved my arms over my head. The wind seemed to buoy me up and carry me with it and I felt gay and free and part of the night, drawing all the music I wanted from the sound of the wind in the trees and the thrum of my pulse.

My mother gave us no very clear lead about people. She was often reckless when she ought to have been careful and timid when boldness would have paid better, like many who are both warm-hearted and sensitive to rebuff. Anything grand and authoritative alarmed her. ('What kind of a lord is he?' she asked once of an expected visitor. 'A viscount.' 'Oh dear, how dreadful!' A baron she might have swallowed.) But the simple and the needy, and such as Salvation Army lassies—always treated to tea with a boiled egg—these she took straight to her heart, particularly if they had any tale of misery to unfold. Once when my father, the protecting barrier, was away from home, a woman sought her out with a tale of woe and wrong so shocking that none of it could be repeated to me or Yda. We met her however and did not forget the glazed look or the swollen parched lips, which she cooled at tea-time by dabbing them with milk from her saucer. Dr. Williamson was called in to see this new protégée and prescribe for her, but alone afterwards with my mother he turned to her, appalled: 'Where did you find that terrible woman?' She borrowed my mother's precious fountain pen and I was sent to ask her for it. I found my way, not easily, to a very old cottage in a little pocket of seventeenth-century Aberdeen which had

been overlooked when the surrounding streets and ter-
races were rebuilt in the end of the eighteenth century.
The garden was a mass of weeds and creepers, wild roses
and honeysuckle. I knocked timidly at a half-open door.
An immediate rustle and scuffle within showed that I had
been observed. After a time I knocked again. There was
a long silence and I went away without the pen.

After such episodes as this my mother would sigh and
say: 'I have learnt my lesson this time.' But I do not think
that she ever did learn it, although when an unsuitable
Irish cousin appeared in Aberdeen she managed to be
cautious for our sakes. This cousin was the famous baby
that was carried in the carpet bag, the gipsy's child,
already mentioned. She had grown up to be an athlete of
distinction, held the British women's championship in
fencing—or was it javelin throwing?—and just after the
war she came to Aberdeen with a university appointment
of a minor sort. Agitated letters reached my mother from
Aunt Lucie and others in Ireland: 'For Mercy's Sake,
Lily, don't let Sophie get hold of the girls.' I was in my
first year at Aberdeen University and very interested to
see this Irish cousin, who came to tea in a stylish fur coat.
She had a husband, but he happened to be in Africa,
exploring. An invitation to take me to a Shaw play was
left floating in mid-air, and my mother sat like an iceberg
(hard work for her) through the whole afternoon. When
Sophie left the town, which she did before very long, she
wrote my mother a sardonic note of thanks for her
cousinly reception. She soon made a name for herself as a
pilot of considerable daring and skill, at a time when very
few women flew at all. Word came—the communica-
tion system in my mother's family never failed—that she
had crashed in America and was badly hurt; had divorced

the explorer; had married a baronet—or perhaps he was only a knight. In a club in London in the late nineteen-twenties, I heard her discussed, her charm and vitality and her gifts, and trickling through the conversation a suggestion of warning, something not unlike the voice of Aunt Lucie saying: 'For Mercy's Sake, don't let Sophie get hold of the girls.' A year or two after this I was shocked to see a paragraph in *The Times* announcing her death. She had fallen down the stairs of a tram in the Old Kent Road.

Cousin Sophie was an eye-opener for us. Earlier there had been Maggie, a great eye-opener. She had come as successor to Helen Marshall who felt shortly after the summer at Newtonmore that cooking and cleaning in the manse was no way to win the war. So she went to a munition factory in Glasgow and Maggie came from a farm on Donside. She was sixteen, a dark-haired, dark-eyed girl, short and as round as a barrel. When Betsy came on Monday to wash she observed Maggie with silent disapproval, took my mother apart, shook her head many times and uttered a number of cryptic achs and ochs. As a result of this my mother wrote to Maggie's parents to ask if they thought it wise that their daughter should be away from home. To my surprise, she told me to go to Maggie in the kitchen one day and ask her very seriously if she were *quite well*. The little secretive tub lifted herself up rather awkwardly from replacing a bucket under the table and after a moment or two turned, flashing me so strange a look from her sloe-black eyes that I have never ceased to see it and to wonder what exactly she meant to tell me with that look. Her words which followed when she glanced away again were entirely disconnected with that message whatever it may have been, for she just said she was brawly. A few days later, very few days in all after her arrival, her Thursday half-day fell due, but when ten o'clock came round no Maggie had returned to the house. My parents immediately guessed that she had decided to go home without either giving notice or waiting for the answer to my mother's letter. To make sure my mother went up to her bedroom at the top of the attic stairs, and found that Maggie had never gone out at all, but was lying on her bed, far advanced in labour. My father went hot-foot to the nearest telephone, my mother to the kitchen to make tea and boil kettles of water. Soon a nurse and a medical student arrived in an ambulance. The baby, a boy, was born about midnight, and a surprisingly thin Maggie, rolled tight in hospital blankets, disappeared on a stretcher into the ambulance a little later. My mother took quite a time to recover from the shock of this, and did not go to see Maggie in hospital, but she sent her a present of fruit and some garment for the child. Maggie wrote to thank her, a little note that I remember well, grammatical, correctly spelt, in a faultless copybook hand. She said: 'I hope God will forgive me for I can never forgive myself.' This was very touching, yet remembering the look in her eyes, anything but forlorn, I think that she may have learnt how to forgive herself in time.

As children we went rarely to the cinema, largely owing to my father's desire not to make it difficult for other parents in the congregation who viewed the influence of the cinema with distrust—'lest by any means this liberty of his became a stumbling-block to them that are weak.' But when we stayed with Aunt Helen in Glasgow we had more freedom and saw a French film of the Fall of Troy. Aphrodite appeared in person as Helen and Paris embraced in a garden laid out on the model of Versailles, lifted her draped arm in front of the lovers, and when she lowered it (wonders!) they had disappeared, and were next seen riding in a sea-shell drawn by a team of doves. I had seen this and perhaps three other films when *The Birth of a Nation* came to His Majesty's Theatre and the whole upper school trooped down to see it one afternoon. This passed over my head as history, but the verisimilitude of the film was almost unbearable to my raw and impressionable mind. I still remember many of the scenes as clearly as I remember the butcher boy who fell beneath the cart. I was the dog that barked at the cat on the screen, and barked again in his sleep night after night. When the dog guessed that he had been cheated probably he never wanted to go to the cinema again, and I scarcely wanted to return after seeing *The Birth of a Nation*, so painful was the fever of mind in which it left me. The film was all pretence and I was alive, and yet I could not help thinking that the people on the screen were really alive while I was merely a stuffed thing able to sit and watch and understand.

From this spiritual dilemma I turned for comfort to Ralph Waldo Emerson and learnt many of his starriest passages by heart. Elsa had told me about Emerson, as she had told me about the Brontës too. If we shared a bedroom we indulged in a *nuit blanche* together, and the whole of *Jane Eyre* had been retold to me in immense detail in a ghostly whisper through one of these treasured nights. For a happiness entirely out of my reach, the happiness of deeds and emotions in a world of people integrated by some secret that I did not know—a world where mothers prepared their sons for battle and girls flung themselves over precipices—Emerson offered an

alternative within my reach, so it seemed, spiritual pos-
session of everything most desirable. 'See to it only that
thyself is here; and art and nature, hope and fate, friends,
angels and the Supreme Being shall not be absent from
the chamber where thou sittest.' I had to take that on
trust, but other passages in the copy of the essays by my
bed, I could underline because I knew them to be true.
'We cannot approach beauty. Its nature is like opaline
doves'-neck lustres, hovering and evanescent. Herein it
resembles the most excellent things which all have their
rainbow character, defying all attempts at appropriation
and use. What else did Jean Paul Richter signify, when
he said to music, "Away! away! thou speakest to me of
things which in all my endless life I have not found and
shall not find." ' That was plain enough, and music constantly pierced me to the quick, but unlike the cinema it
left no sickness and misery behind. I could suffer from it
and remain in command of myself. My mother to the
end of her life cried 'Away! Away!' to certain composers,
but for me in time all distress passed, and when I hear
certain favourite pieces now and remember how I felt
listening to them forty years ago, then I know that life
has both satisfied something and killed something. From
one point of view this book is an attempt to discover for
myself what it killed and what it is that makes youthful
perceptions seem so acute while still so undeveloped. For
almost all the senses except possibly the sense of smell
improve with use and experience. It may be that the
reactions of children appear powerful because children
themselves are weak. Experience has not yet provided
them with an answer back to anything. As a little girl,
and even as an adolescent, I had no pith; every puff of
wind flattened me to the ground. Like someone suffering

from congenital and chronic nervous breakdown—because there was as yet no nervous build-up—I lacked that cohesion of mind and body without which the eye alone or the ear alone takes the full brunt of circumstances, and even the noise of a banging door can be quite unbearable or the motion of a caterpillar spell disaster.

The hardiness that comes with age and experience is seldom bought at too high a price. I could face living again through most of my life but not the nights of torture from over-excitement, the thrashing through the green brain of a new idea, a new friendship, a play or a stanza of poetry, knives in the hubs of chariot wheels which never stopped rolling through the hours of darkness (so much longer at fifteen than at fifty). And yet if one can preserve one's sanity with it, how important is insomnia! Without the extra years it gives for thought, only the intellectual giants can draw level with their experience. Even in those early days it was not lying and thinking that I dreaded, but lying and thinking the same thing. The mere habit of lying awake was already well established before we went to Aberdeen. Long after I had been put to bed at Berwick I lay listening to the strange and lonely sound of the curfew tolling; or in the middle of the night my burning eyes did not dare to leave the serpents beckoning from the top of my mother's wardrobe, until daylight turned them back into the handles of tennis rackets. But when I was in my teens and examinations approached, my parents grew concerned about my wakefulness and my father refused to play chess with me when I had finished my homework in case it stimulated my mind too much. Instead of chess he took me for ten or fifteen minutes' brisk walk in the fresh air, and very fresh air it was, in the empty streets beneath the crowded

sky. But I think that this made me livelier still at bedtime.

Thinking in circles, coming back and back to the same
thought, that at its best grows tedious and at its worst
becomes madness. From this time I discovered that happiness for me consisted in either breaking new ground or
discovering my old thoughts in a different shape. 'And
happiness . . . what is it?' wrote that wise man and great
artist from New York to his son Willie in Ireland. 'I say
it is neither virtue nor pleasure nor this thing or that, but
simply *growth*. We are happy when we are growing. It
is the primal law of all nature and the universe, and literature and art are the cosmic movements working in the
conscious mind.'[1]

The importance of novels and of films originated a good
deal in the difficulty of finding out about grown-up
people. There was a far greater barrier between the young
and the old than there is now, and grown-up people
talked very impersonally, about Home Rule for Ireland,
or life in the Colonies. The only form of personal talk to
be relied upon was about illness, which was terrifying—
it seemed so easy to have everything wrong. But my
mother formed the exception with her Irish recollections,
and her frank comments upon the task of being a minister's wife. We knew how tired she was at the end of a
day, 'worn to a ravelling' and 'past herself', and we suspected that in some way in spite of all her religious faith
she felt balked, as she smoothed her neck with her hands
and sighed, saying: 'Oh my dears, I am getting old.' Of
marriage itself her views were pungent yet obscure.
'Your dear father is an angel,' she often said in a way that

[1] J. B. Yeats, *Letters to His Son*, edited by Joseph Hone (Faber &
Faber).

carried complete conviction. She adored children and had never been able to resist the temptation to have just one more and one more, but all the same we were frequently warned to avoid matrimony as a hotbed of troubles. When we were actually grown-up she began to think that it would be better for us to risk the troubles than to end up with neither chick nor child. But often she doubted her own judgment on this. She made a last general comment in her ninetieth year, a few weeks before she died (which she did with the nobility and beauty of one of the saints). 'I really have come to think very poorly of married life. I tell Aphra [her unmarried sister a few years younger than herself] she is very fortunate; she doesn't know how fortunate she is.' I reminded her of the old saying that marriage is like a bird-cage, and the birds that are in want to get out, while those that are out want to get in. My mother: 'No bird in its senses would want to get *inside* a cage.'

As we grew up my mother presented us with one rule of conduct. Never, never, she said, look round at a man in the street or in any public place at all, and never speak to a stranger. This was a law of the Medes and Persians. (So Biblical was our early background that we regarded the Romans as upstarts in law-making, and always harked back to the Medes and Persians. And while in parenthesis let me pay tribute to the prettiness of nineteenth-century speech, so much more adorned than ours with proverbs and traditional phrases. 'The old dog for the rough road and the pup for the path,' my mother used to say as she gladly and impulsively relieved me of some task that weighed upon me, and when I thanked her she would assure me that she found it merely a dolly-idle-stitch. We were apples and nuts to her. For many generations in her family such gracious sayings had passed down from mother to daughter.)

There was a theory in the family that I was very thin-skinned and should be spared distressing and alarming talk, but I believe that this was nonsense, and that I was always tougher and bolder than my sisters—although that may not be saying a great deal. Yda suffered much from fears which were not dissipated at all by my mother's warnings about men. She hated travelling alone. Once she had the misfortune to travel to Glasgow on the same train as a team of cheerful Glasgow foot-ballers returning from playing a match in Aberdeen. One of them spied the golden-haired lass sitting alone in her compartment, and they all came crowding to look at her and to try in their lumbering way to coax a smile or an encouraging word. As soon as they broke rank to debate upon their failure Yda made a dash for the corridor and fled along, like Florimell 'and eke through feare as white as whales bone', until she met the guard. He, kind man, conducted her soothingly to a first-class compartment and locked her in and presently brought along the cap-tain of the team to apologize humbly for annoying her.

This was a transitional time for girls. We had so little experience it was hardly fair to send us about without protection, and yet with the world moving the way it was, not to be able to travel alone after one was fifteen seemed absurd. Yet Yda had another alarming experience when she went by herself to stay with the Willie cousins at Birkenhead and asked to be directed to Park Road South when she arrived at Lime Street Station in Liver-pool. There was another Park Road besides the Birken-head one and it was only when she found herself descend-ing from a tram in Chinatown that Yda realized her mistake. When at last, much shaken by this, she arrived at the right house, the quiet and respectable suburban villa in Birkenhead, Uncle Willie 'chaffed her unmercifully' as they said in those days, and continued his unmerciful chaffing for the rest of her visit. This is a word less used now, and really less often required, for the wise have grown shy of making fun of the foolish, as the high-born have ceased to lord it over the commoners and the rich to exploit the poor.

Fear of the perils of this life always bulked larger in our thoughts than fear of punishment in the next. Even our parents had not been brought up to fear damnation and it played no part in the teaching that they gave us. Or perhaps it is truer to say that the idea of damnation as something very alarming not necessarily in the next world did enter into their teaching, but not hell fire. The worst thing was scandal. If anyone went to the dogs, it was scandal, and going to the dogs meant getting involved with low characters, losing an honest means of living, cheating and stealing, living in fear of the police and in danger of imprisonment. Going to the dogs might also mean taking to drink and gambling and betting, but harlotry did not exist for me outside the Bible and I had put my hair up before I knew that it was not obsolete. The only member of our family whom I could picture going to the dogs was Archie—now an honorary Doctor of Divinity of his old university—because in spite of teaching in Sunday School and going twice a Sunday to church, he was full of sociability and high spirits and loved dances and once ran down a dentist with his toboggan in Kings Gate. The dentist suffered a broken leg and a police constable called to see Archie, a very alarming episode which passed off better than I ever hoped, for the dentist and all his family succumbed at once to Archie's friendliness and remorse and high spirits and became his allies from that time on.

Then Mr. Asquith arrived in Aberdeen as Lord Rector of the university. The students met him at the station, removed the cabby from the seat of his cab, the horse from the shafts, and themselves performed the task of cabby and horse. Afterwards they broke the cab into little bits so that everyone could have a share, and Archie returned home with a piece of leather and some horsehair stuffing. The following week the *Illustrated London News* arrived from Great-aunt Agnes with one page heavily margined with multiple pencil lines. It was a photograph of the rag at its height with the cab practically submerged in the sea of revellers. In the centre of the picture was Archie, grinning his wonderful unmistakable grin. It was a shocking affair.

Archie's unquenchable spirits made a great contribution to our family life. My father bore the endless minor calamities that befell us with patience; my mother though often dismayed and stricken for a little, fought back bravely, but Archie's reaction was entirely different—he would be, as we said then, tickled to death. Sometimes this annoyed the person picking up the fragments, but as a rule everyone was caught up in the tornado of laughter which he let loose. One very busy evening when a double bed had to be made up and aired in a hurry for an unexpected visitor, my mother sent Archie up with a stone hot-water bottle, not knowing that one had already been put in the bed. Archie shot the bottle down between the sheets with such force that both exploded, drenching the mattress and all the bedclothes. This was almost more than my mother could bear, but Archie laughed until he was too weak to stand on his feet, and then until he was too weak to sit upright, and we all joined in. Archie's fun took many forms, including leaping from behind doors, or catching my ankles as I went upstairs, and owing to this I was sometimes struck with panic even when he was not in the house. The first days about the house after jaundice and my long fast I suddenly thought perhaps Archie was upon me, and started to run along the passage upstairs, but fell at once owing to the feebleness of my legs. This sort of fear revealed (for my mother came hurrying to pick me up and ask what on earth had happened) made him very penitent and solicitous. We lived in an atmosphere preternaturally free from rancour, although in our ignorance of life we did not think so. When my father broke it to me one summer that he could not afford to pay my subscription to the school tennis club, so that I must do without tennis that year, I felt so aggrieved that I harangued him upon the unwisdom of this form of economy. He neither justified himself nor reproved me but waited until I had finished and said gently: 'Yes, dearie.' I flounced off to school but before I had reached the Den Burn my bravado had vanished and I felt struck to the heart. I ran back to fling my arms round him and hug him, and then rushed off again without a word, though no word was needed.

No lucky star, no silver spoon in the mouth, no caul upon the head at birth can equal the advantage of being born at the tail end of a large family. Parents grow calmer and more indulgent, and the older children guide, stimulate, pet and encourage. I had Archie's brilliant interpretation of life as high comedy, and Jack's piano-playing and his example of a studious life. He roped me in to help him, which I was proud to do by reading Thucydides

aloud in English while he followed the text in Greek.
Elsa, voyaging through strange seas of thought, beckoned
me to join her, and showed always a deep sense of
responsibility for my education in matters quite outside
the school curriculum. When she graduated and went
south, she asked one of her friends, Tibbie Smith, still
at the university, to come and talk to me sometimes.
With great kindness this girl, who was seven or eight
years my senior, spared an evening from time to time,
and drank cocoa with me in the bedroom I had inherited
from Elsa, and told me about hormones and the influence
of mind over matter.

Between Edward and me and Yda the two-way traffic
of affection coursed in the fresh and artless way undis-
coverable in this world except between siblings in childhood. We were too close to know how close. I see myself and Edward on the front lawn of the manse, like two
little kids from the fold, dunting and pushing bony forehead to bony forehead and chanting inanely: 'We are
fiends, aren't we? We are fiends!' For we thought it
amazingly funny that the word friend spelt without an
'r' turned into fiend. A photograph still exists of me with
both hands tight round Yda's neck and Yda as cheerful
as Porphyria, since the photographer had said: 'Can't you
make her sit still just one minute?' (As Aunt Christina
said: Baby would prance round.)

In the clustered growth of six children born in twelve
years there was bound to be a battle of personal tastes and
ideas, but if we broke out in criticism of one another, my
mother was up in arms, the powerful arms of Scripture.
My father remained as a rule neutral but his own blandness
rebuked our irritation with one another. 'My dears, little
birds in their nests agree.' It may not be quite true, but

we knew the shocking consequences when they dis-
agreed and perhaps took warning. I always considered
fault-finding by the family of the family could co-exist
with the belief that we were all inevitably and justifiably
ourselves, and so above any serious criticism from the
outside world. Thus we reproduced in miniature the self-
satisfaction of a small nation that will stand neither rebuke
nor interference. 'Horribly good-looking and horribly
stuck-up,' was the description that my contemporary
Olive Lindsay gave of my brothers. But to me Archie
was simply Archie, a great big fellow, high-spirited, soft-
hearted, lazy and gifted, teasing and full of laughter;
Elsa a Nordic goddess of great dignity and inscrutability,
and Jack a model of propriety and achievement, quiet,
elegant, and the most studious of us all. When an elder
of the church, half-joking, called Archie a young scally-
wag, and a friend from England found Jack conven-
tional, I resented both these comments deeply.

CHAPTER NINE

When the Reed Spoke

With so many children, so little money and so much to do inside and outside the home, it was a wonder that both my parents did not suffer more from frustration. It was a real event for them to buy a book which was not a work of theology or a text-book. I remember my mother's pleasure in possessing an autobiography of Mrs. Booth-Clibborn, La Maréchale, General Booth's daughter, and what a plunge it was for my father to buy Francis Thompson's Poems. With leisure my mother would have been as great a reader of books as my father. Her very attitude as she read a book showed the sharpness of the appetite that it fed. Her long fingers curved round the spine almost fiercely and made me think of a spider embracing its catch. She never forgot a story that impressed her and *Trilby*, the wild oats of her youthful reading, made a lifelong mark on her. An oil painting, a portrait of my grandfather, the father-in-law whose admiration and kindness had so supported her in the Liverpool days, passed into her keeping with other remnants of 18 Devonshire Road when she was in her late eighties. A grandson unrolled the canvas before her unprepared eyes, creating an emotional agitation which she could describe only by saying: 'My dears, I felt that I was Trilby and he was Svengali.' I think that he was one of the first people to do justice to my mother's gift for writing—used only in letters. When she wrote to him from Fort Etna describing the spring, he pasted the letter inside a volume of Richard Jefferies.

Even in middle age she could not resist a novel, and sucked the heart out of it in less time than seemed possible. We went to tea once with Oliver de Selincourt, then a lecturer at Aberdeen University. My mother picked up a recent novel by H. G. Wells, while our host fetched the teapot, and she did not quite take her eyes off the book until the end of our visit. Oliver offered to lend it to her, but she said: 'Oh no thank you, I have really finished it,' and on the way home she gave me the outline of the plot and a criticism of the book as a whole. Her taste was infallible as far as prose went, for it had been formed upon close and continuous reading of the Authorized Version of the Bible. But Moody and Sankey weakened her judgment for verse, and all her life she was liable to be carried away by a jingle if she could match the sentiments with her own.

Nosing about in Bissett's bookshop one day during the war, she picked up Compton Mackenzie's *Sinister Street*, Volume One. Mr. Bissett, seeing her looking at it and probably knowing from experience what a rapid reader she was, quickly said that a missionary home from China had described it to him as the best novel she had ever read. I particularly remember that it was China, and how that gave the report a high intellectual value. My mother brought it home and handed it to me with this recommendation. I read it with fascination and astonishment, fortunately before my mother had time to look her choice over more thoroughly. When she did she expressed some doubt about the missionary's outlook, but it was too late to do anything else and I think that she was almost as fascinated as I was. From *Sinister Street* I went on to read *Paradise Lost*. The Milton we had read at school, *L'Allegro* and *Il Penseroso* and a few sonnets, had passed over my head, but the lines that haunted Michael Fane—

> *Thick as Autumnal Leaves*
> *That strow the Brooks in Vallombrosa*

—acted as a bait which led me far into *Paradise Lost* and thereby prepared my ear for *Samson Agonistes* when it became a set book at school. I learnt hundreds of lines from both by heart and chanted them to the waves on Balgownie beach.

I had returned to Mr. Mackie's school as I entered my teens, but Mr. Mackie himself was mortally ill and died before long. Early in the war Margaret Thirde was appointed headmistress. The school itself showed every sign of mortal sickness and only a very brave woman would have taken the post, but Miss Thirde was brave, eager and energetic, full of ideas. She was one of the advance guard among those educationalists who disapproved of teaching girls as if they were boys, in the expectation that later on they would be indistinguishable from men. Cooking and sewing, singing and dancing and drawing were now given much more prominence in our time-tables, and we did in fact pass our external examinations without doing a stroke of bookwork any afternoon of the week. Miss Thirde cared almost as much for the appearance of a classroom as its uses. 'What sort of homes

are you girls going to make?' she asked in despair, looking at the disorder of chairs and desks and books, and then
turning her dark quick eyes to the mantelpiece where an
unhappy tulip squirmed in its pot: 'I suppose that piece of
vegetation is intended to be ornamental.' One girl who
could do fine lettering was set to make us a motto to
hang upon the wall.

Her voice was ever soft,
Gentle, and low, an excellent thing in woman.

Miss Thirde herself taught English, but her adminis-
trative duties so often kept her, that many of our lessons
consisted of reading on aloud by ourselves, a method that
led us into difficulties, particularly in the *Faerie Queene*,
until someone said firmly: 'We can't be meant to read
THIS aloud' and then with general relief we skipped to
the next episode. I revered Miss Thirde, I doted upon her,
and no wonder, for she supplied an element of drama
otherwise quite lacking at school. Life jerked out of its
rut the moment that she came into the room. She went
faster to the point than anyone I had met before. She
even went faster on her feet than any other adult, along
the bleak passages of the old school and up the long flight
of stairs, while her gown, slipping off her shoulders,
swept the ground behind her. The quick impatient movement as she hitched it into place comes back vividly.
Everything about her comes back as fresh and clear as if
it had only happened the other day. So I remember
blushing as she reproved me for arriving at school on a
mild spring day without gloves—as a point of etiquette
—although I had only a few minutes' walk along deserted
streets from my home. One November afternoon, a day
of strong yet mild winds and low yet restrained cloud,

she sent me with a pound note to buy some stationery at MacKeggie's shop. On my return I gave her the change in the big classroom on the left of the front door. Everyone had gone home. She put the money on the mantelpiece and when I returned later to the empty classroom to collect my satchel it was still there. I picked up the tower of silver to carry it to Miss Thirde in her room, and on the way I realized that one of the six half-crowns was missing. Such moments of alarm like an acid burn every detail of the time and scene into the memory, and so as I think of it, I am there again in the empty, unlit shell of the school, climbing the worn stone staircase to Miss Thirde's little room at the end of the landing beyond the science laboratory. I know again the sudden contrast of the soft Indian rug on to which I stepped as I handed her the short change and told her my discovery. I knew that she had not counted the money when I first gave it to her. Miss Thirde sat silent, her eyes on the money in the palm of her hand and her thick dark brows drawn together in thought, one of them always up-tilted at the temple. I realized that she was neither worried nor vexed nor suspicious; she was just thinking. Then her face changed, the brows cleared, she lifted her eyes and smiled her brilliant smile. 'Of course,' she said, 'I gave half a crown to Miss Milne.' (Oh Miss Milne, the caretaker who lived in the basement; dark, unsmiling, dressed in black alpaca, felt-slippered, carrying the little brush and pan which seemed to be her only implements for cleaning those huge old houses.)

Before I left school Miss Thirde married the widower-father of one of her youngest boarders and went to live on an orange farm north of Johannesburg. I saw her once again in London ten years later. She had no children of her own and died in middle age after a long illness, and I find it hard to accept the oblivion of time and the grave for someone so real and so gifted; but her achievements were particularly intangible. I dreamt of her recently as she was in her twenties and dressed in a sober navy serge dress with a square-cut neck. Sitting on a sofa we talked more easily together than ever in life. I wish we had discussed her production of *The Land of Heart's Desire* as the school play. It took Aberdeen by storm, and the day that we began to learn the fairy song is cherished in my mind as no other day at school. Sadie Rennett—chosen for the part of the fairy child, which she fitted beyond admiration—stood in front of the singing class with the book in her hands, and read the words to us, line by line, in her small, soft voice. There was a murmur of uneasiness. Someone questioned 'gates of the day'—wasn't it dawn? Before she had finished I left my place and took the book from her hands—bossy, peremptory, in a strange state. Often sitting upon those benches with a notebook I had been handed a stone or a serpent: Dryden one day, Ella Wheeler Wilcox another. I was never less prepared for a wave from an unknown sea of poetry and beauty. It broke over me, lifted me up and flung me down on the shores of heaven.

But I heard a reed of Coolaney say. . . .

I could not keep the book (it was Miss Thirde's) but I found out when Sadie would copy out her part, and I went and fetched it from her house one evening and returned it at school the next morning. I never mentioned my excitement to Miss Thirde or discussed Yeats with anyone then, nor did I understand how much of my emotion was due to the fierce battle in my own heart

153

between my Christian upbringing and my intuitive pantheism. Christianity repudiated so much that I cherished.

> *The wan moon is setting behind the white wave,*
> *And time is setting with me, O.*

That was true for Burns, and might be true for me or for anyone. I could not deliver melancholy over to the Devil. It was good that 'Shakespeare was on the side of the angels' (though I thought my father patronizing when he said so) yet I jibbed at the thought of his going any further than that. Shakespeare with the faith of Bunyan, the idea seemed crude and intolerable. It tested my belief as nothing else could, and found something false and weak at the foundations.

If I had been asked to name one person further from such perplexities than another I should instantly have chosen my father. To him the dancing figures of *The Land of Heart's Desire*—'Shaking their milk-white feet in a ring'—so like the dancing children of heaven and hell in my first remembered dream, must always have belonged to outer darkness. Yet three months before his death he wrote to me:

'Talking of dreams, I have some extraordinary clear and sensible ones. After dipping into *Puck of Pook's Hill* I dreamt of seeing a man standing looking seaward on the last Scottish cliff and killed (!) by a Celtic woman named Mograbalita because she felt he was triumphing over Gaeldom and the ancient culture. There were endless delays in getting witnesses to the inquiry, trains breaking down or blocked on single lines. I felt when I woke up first that I could have made a really excellent story out of its varied events, but they went like the early dew.'
The heart—that 'unseen seat of life and sentient target of

death'—felt the approach of its supreme crisis. In sleep
when the mind can listen, it passed the message on, but I
did not understand it, nor did my father, although he
made that strange little gesture of embarrassment (!)
perhaps even of fear. Physical death was far from our
thoughts, but from the time of that dream my ideas
about him changed, and I saw that he knew about my
conflict from his own experience. How the imagination
of Yeats himself would have taken fire at the picture of
the man looking seaward on the last Scottish cliff.

CHAPTER TEN

Finishing in 1918

To our cousins 'The Willies' in Birkenhead, we were known privately as 'The Poor Johns', and they thought it awful to be us. We thought it pretty hard lines to be them, although we too forebore to mention it. Not that we despised money, nothing like that at all, but Uncle Willie and Aunt Lilian seemed severe to us, and we were sensitive and did not like the way they made fun of children. But I gladly put up with their mockery for the sake of staying with Hugh and Evelyn and Andrew, the three older children. In the very fine hot summer of 1911 Edward and Yda and I spent August with them in a big house on the shores of Lake Ullswater. At ten I was not nearly as tall as Evelyn who was only three months my senior, for we northerners did our growing late, and the grown-ups commented perpetually on my stunted appearance. All children had their dose of snubbing in those days and I must have shown that I was in need of a double dose. On a walk from Howtown to Patterdale—an outing that most parents today would avoid to save themselves the torture of keeping the fussy modern child happy under a hot sun on a long walk—I plunged into telling Evelyn the whole of one of Dorothea Moore's historical romances. The Elizabethan child-heroine was punished, not with a stick like my cousins, but by being given two chapters of the prophet Habakkuk to learn by heart. Aunt Lilian overheard this as we walked along and named me Habakkuk from that day on. I did not understand why I was pilloried for this until I heard her explaining my nickname before me to visitors. I had shown myself a proper little Philistine by chattering away a lot of nonsense and distracting Evelyn's attention through some of the most beautiful scenery in England. Secretly I thought the Lake District not a patch on the Highlands, but I saw that Aunt Lilian had something on her side. I could not think badly of her because of the charming way that she called Evelyn *Sis*, saying in her warm vibrant voice: 'Is anything wrong, Sis? Has your sailor-boy gone to sea and left you?' I admired too the ideas she had, for hen houses and dish-washing machines and gymnastic apparatus in the nursery. Money was used to give her family more scope and I particularly liked one example of this in Evelyn's thick black woollen stockings made with a separate place for the big toe, so that she could waggle her big toes freely when she walked. The only sad thing about that holiday occurred near the end, on a sultry picnic in a wood by a waterfall when my store of romances had run dry. I caught on to the idea of teasing and selected Hugh as my victim, although he had always been kind and friendly to me. I paid dearly for my silliness and ingratitude, for I lost his confidence for ever.

As for Uncle Willie, if anyone had a natural right to make fun of us, he had, because of his genuine grandness. We noticed with deep appreciation that he knew exactly whom to tip and when to do it and how much to give them. To simplify this supremely difficult accomplishment he kept a great deal of his wonderful money loose in his trouser pocket, whereas my father carried his in a worn leather purse and knew just what he would find there when he opened it and let the coins slide to view on to the leather tray that closed it. Uncle Willie always changed into evening dress for dinner and wore an eye-glass dangling on a black silk ribbon, and looked aristo-cratic and calm whatever happened, not unlike C. E. Brock's idea of Mr. Darcy.

Three years after the Ullswater holiday we were in-vited to join the Willies again, this time to go to the Isle of Man. Great crowds at the stations made travelling even more disagreeable than usual, and a few days after we had arrived in Birkenhead a very strange thing happened. Edward and I were sitting with the three older cousins in the schoolroom after children's supper, when Uncle Willie walked in with his table napkin still in his hand. He had been called to the telephone (a new and awesome invention) in the middle of dinner. He said: 'We shan't be going to the Isle of Man, children. England is at war with Germany.'

So we five older ones were packed off to Aunt Lilian's bachelor brother who lived in the family house near Chester, and there we spent the first month of the war. Uncle Tom went to his office in Manchester for most of the week, and left us with the housekeeper and the groom. We never set eyes on the housekeeper but the groom took full charge and planned many outings in the trap. Hugh had a shotgun and we all had fishing rods, and no one cared in the least when we went to bed, so we played Steps on the lawn after supper until it was too dark to see. I remember no newspapers and no talk of the war. When Uncle Tom came home we went walking in the fields with him and watched him slaughter the thistles with the blade at the end of his walking stick. Only on the day that we visited Beeston Castle do I remember emerging for a few minutes from this seclusion. We saw motor cars with flags on them and heard strangers greet and question one another in an unconventional way. I went up to Hugh and said: 'What's happening?' 'How do I know? I suppose there is a big battle going on in France.' He spoke as of a new Crecy or Waterloo, and it was hard for us to understand the smallest part of the design of modern warfare. We had been brought up to think that progress (which was manifest) meant that man had evolved past anything more violent and unpleasant than a coal strike at home or a riot in distant parts. Anything so contrary to all beliefs and expectations as war might last a few weeks but not long enough to postpone the opening of school in September, so that we could stay a little longer with our cousins.

Evelyn and I slept together in a four-poster bed in a room where Queen Elizabeth I had once slept. After our speculations about the battle in France I was moved to talk about the end of the world, as I had been taught to expect it by my mother, a fervent student of the prophetic books of the Bible and the Apocalypse. I was surprised that it seemed an unfamiliar field to Evelyn. My story was so detailed and my own belief so firm that she was impressed and even worried—in spite of my placing Armageddon at the immensely far-off date of 1940. (This was fixed by a book of my mother's on the pyramids.) I wrote to my mother in Aberdeen to ask for particulars in order to convince Evelyn, who was after all as good a Presbyterian as I was myself—if an English Presbyterian could ever be in the same class as a Scottish one. My letter may have put my mother in an awkward position, or it may be that my father, who did not share her views, intervened. In any case, no chapter and verse was given for me to pass on, and doubt began to trickle into my own mind. I slept the easier for thinking that after all I might not have to face the dreaded ordeal of refusing to take the Mark of the Beast on my forehead. But my mother never lost her interest or belief in the prophetical books. Not many years before she died she wrote me a characteristic letter. 'Elsa wrote to Mary Kelly to ask why she got no Univ. voting papers. M.K. replies Mr. Atlee and his wretches[1] have done away with the univ seats altogether. There seems utter confusion. Students of prophecy see that we are now in the time of the toes of Daniel's Image, "part of iron and part of clay", Dan ii, 40. The veracity and accuracy of Daniel's prophecies have been amply verified. Will Lord Vansittart be listened to on Communist China in to-day's *Times*?'

When the First World War broke out Edward was nearly seventeen. He had neither the prodigious vitality and jovial spirits of Archie, nor the scholarly and musical gifts of Jack, but was a very serious and gentle boy. He inherited my mother's skill with plants and flowers, and could turn his hand to many things, carpentry, cooking, sewing, sketching, always setting himself to perfect whatever he undertook. His tidiness was unnatural, yet most acceptable in a large household such as ours. Now as he grew up and there were no more games in the attic or hide-and-seek in the garden, he came nearer to his

[1] My mother's description of the Labour Party, not M.K.'s.

parents and Elsa, leaving me behind. Steps on the lawn at Uncle Tom's was our last game, and when soon he became a medical student at Aberdeen, I mourned his remoteness. One day I found myself alone in his bedroom and noticed a blue pencil lying on the marble-topped table near his bed. Carelessly, mainly with the itch to see something in blue on the pink and white slab, I picked up the pencil and wrote: 'Don't be grumpy.' Months afterwards my mother told me that Edward had been upset when he noticed it. It echoed the tiffs and criticisms of Fort Etna days, her own childhood. He was already away in Edinburgh training to be an officer in the Royal Field Artillery. I meant some time to apologize and tell him how little, if he did wish to be grumpy, it changed my love for him. He did tend to look on the dark side of life, or perhaps he was the one realist in our family. Forty years later Innes Logan wrote reminding me of 'our beloved Ted, trailing in from school with his books saying disconsolately: "There's always something rotten somewhere." '

By the autumn of 1916, even in the quiet and safety of the manse, the war had settled down upon us like one of the plagues of Egypt, but with no Moses to call it off. Archie had finished his medical studies and joined the R.A.M.C. Jack had been rejected for military service on account of his short sight and was now in the consulate in Copenhagen. Elsa was teaching in Surrey, soon to join the Waacs. In France and Belgium their friends and contemporaries were falling like grass before a scythe, and the course of history was being changed for the worse as never before by any disaster, any conquest or any tyranny. But those of us who survived and were still young had at least the buoyancy of mind that goes with youth and so could come to understand what was happening. Many people who were past their youth in 1914 went through the war trying to believe their senses and failing, and many of them remained intellectually shell-shocked for the rest of their lives. The axiom that the worst never does happen had upheld them so long, it was hard to keep on their feet without it. Indeed, for a long time we had been so secure that the romantic appeal of distant terrors was prodigious. Wolves, waterspouts and vampires were as necessary to us as the salt in our porridge, and we battened on tales of the Great Plague and the Fire of London, and—on Sundays—the Spanish Inquisition. My mother even in her day had a cousin who used to settle down on the window seat of the schoolroom at Fort Etna with Fox's *Book of Martyrs*, saying: 'Oh this is a lovely book. How I should like to be a martyr!' When the *Titanic* went down; when Captain Scott failed to return from the Antarctic, the line between the past and the present, things remote and things at home, tautened for us with a sudden jerk. These were the dreams of the prophetic soul of the wide world. Scott's journals tell the story of shattered complacency: 'We are in a very Queer Street indeed,' he wrote. The accepted pattern of life refused to repeat. Men continued to play their part as before, but found something entirely unmanageable, even malevolent in the elements. Then when the war itself broke the wild beast in the wood proved to be the most dangerous kind of all, a man.

My father found it harder than most to believe what was happening, as was inevitable in this most gentle of Christians, the flower of many generations of followers of the Jesus who had touched the ear of the servant of the High Priest and healed it. He never ceased to pray and hope that the rulers of the warring nations would meet and agree to end the slaughter. When hatred of the Boche ran high he spoke bravely of the Germans, kindly good people, whom he had known from his boyhood when Great-aunt Minnie had taken him and Willie on a tour up the Rhine and to the Black Forest.

If it crossed my mind to join the V.A.D.—as many schoolgirls no older than I did—I never dared to put the thought into words, knowing how much it would alarm my parents. Instead of that I gathered sphagnum moss in sacks upon the moors during our summer holidays, and sent it off to the Red Cross depot in Aberdeen. Then during the rest of the year I went to the depot on Saturday mornings to pick the heather and grass and leaves from piles of dry moss, always of much inferior quality to any that I had gathered. Other workers packed the clean moss into gauze bags. Others sewed the bags up, and they were sent to France as swabs and dressings for the wounded. The moss is very absorbent and was said to have healing virtues. Someone passed round a little hard smooth cake of compressed moss from a German field hospital and told us that the Germans had been gathering the moss in Scotland for many years. It was always being rubbed into us what amateurs we were in the business of modern warfare compared with our enemies, and now we schoolgirls, picking away at our heaps like busy little hens on a midden, tried to catch up on them.

It became easy now to find quiet and solitude in the manse, but now I did not relish it so much. *La Solitude est une belle chose; mais il faut avoir quelqu'un a qui l'on puisse dire—La Solitude est une belle chose*. We edged the little flags backwards and forwards a fraction on the map of the battlefield and waited for letters from the brothers or from grandfather telling of the latest adventure of Uncle Leonard who kept on going down in torpedoed warships and bobbing up again until he was quite accustomed to the experience. Like the old wife in our fairy-tale book, still I sat, and still I span—thoughts not thread —and still I wished for company. Strange company rewarded the patience of the old wife, and rather strange company came to me in the shape of one of Archie's university friends, Bill Gilbert, who had served first with the Guides (the crack regiment of the Punjab Frontier Force) and then with the 53rd Sikhs in Mesopotamia, but now was invalided home. He had stayed with us before the war on his way out to India, and I remembered the flattering patience with which he had listened to my confidences about writing, and the charming present which he had sent me from India, a tiny basket containing a hundred polished but unset moonstones, all different shapes and sizes. My mother remembered that he had no mother of his own, and no brothers or sisters, and how he had warmed at once to her kindness.

Bill Gilbert was not in any sense a Presbyterian. In my eyes his worldliness was so great, his reading and knowledge so wide—it was considerable—he had so much *nous*, and was in all respects so unlike my own family that neither Caoilte tossing his burning hair nor Niamh calling Away come away! could have fascinated me more. He weaned me from Gene Stratton Porter and put me on to O. Henry, and to widen my knowledge of the globe, he gave me Kipling's *From Sea to Sea*. We had never seen any of the cartoons of Bruce Bairnsfather, so he bought us those thin sombre-coloured volumes of the collected cartoons now no more than curiosities of the past. My parents could not accept humour plucked from so much horror, but I saw the war for the first time as factual—noise, blood and filth—and the combatants as men not unlike my brother Archie, dogged and irrepressible and given to unseemly mirth. Bill also persuaded my mother to play the piano again and to please him she got Sinding's 'Marche Grotesque' and the music of *Chu Chin Chow*, then all the rage in London, a city I had never visited. After his hard and lonely upbringing detraction came naturally to him. My Miss Thirde became simply the Thirde Person Singular, and he shocked me by quoting from an experienced uncle that after six years of married life there was nothing left for husband and wife to discuss but the price of butter. As Byron had proved, no one has more glamour for others than a young man who has discovered that there is no glamour left. I can distinguish however, looking back, a touching anxiety that I should not catch up on him too fast. When I wrote to him of reading *Sinister Street* his comment shot back from the Indus valley—'*Sinister Street*, yes indeed, but surely rather a far cry from *The Schönberg-Cotta Family*?' He was the first person to grow annoyed with the distractions, whether feminine or academic or religious, that I permitted to interfere with my destiny. 'I expect you to write your name across the sky.' Although flattering, that was also disconcerting, but his admiration of my mother as a nonpareil gave me unqualified satisfaction, particularly coming from someone who believed in so little.

I found Bill's conversation amusing and stimulating and was pleased to find myself rattling away at the dinner table. Unexpected witticisms popped out of my mouth. I knew nothing about the pleasant effect of a glass of champagne, yet that was just the effect of our visitor. I never dreamt that it could be improper to behave so. Bill went back to London for a time, but asked if he might return before his leave expired, and then to my great chagrin my mother explained that I must agree not to be witty and gay if he came, not, as my father described it, get upon my high horse. It was a great shock to discover the incompetence of my own conscience and I certainly checked myself. But my mother was in two minds about the part she played in passing on my father's strictures. When I said my laconic farewell to Bill at the end of this second visit she ran out of the dining-room after me and kissed me kindly before I started off for school.

I took for granted that my father was right and that I had behaved without decorum, but because it was so hard to see how I had done this, his opinion gave me a new shyness and *gaucherie* in mixed company. He thought his daughters as rare as they were precious to him personally, and lived in mortal fear of our making unwise marriages. My mother was saved much anxiety by the assumption that marriage could only seem alarming and distasteful to us, and this innocent viewpoint made my father feel all the more responsible. And in addition to this he was exceedingly ambitious for his daughters. No education was too good for them and no future too distinguished. He was one of the very few men I have known who genuinely believed in the equality of the sexes.

Edward too was feeling his way to ties outside the family. When his training in the Field Artillery took him to Dorset he met Vernon Ory, who traced his ancestry back to the famous French crusader. The Orys had an only daughter of seventeen called Peggy, clever, good and distractingly pretty. Edward was very much torn

how to divide his leave between the manse in Aberdeen
and the Orys' house in London, where he was made as
welcome as one of the family. My mother urged him to
spend all the time that he could with his new friends,
because she saw that it gave him happiness, and she
thought of nothing else. But Edward never became engaged to Peggy Ory. She was still at school and he was
only a medical student, in the army for the duration of
the war. When they saw him off from Victoria for the
front Mrs. Ory said: 'Oh aren't you going to kiss Peggy
good-bye?' and Edward replied gravely: 'I don't think
she would like it.' This was in the beginning of 1918 and
he was twenty, six feet tall but looking less than his age.
But for the shortness of his ash-blond hair, which had
vexed him so as a boy with its crisp curls, he resembled
no one more than the page of Nicholas of Tolentino in
the Rout of San Romano. He was as beautiful as that
and the same lambent purity and purpose shone from his
eyes and his whole face. We were told that his fellow
officers grew self-conscious in his hearing, if their conversation turned bawdy or foolish. They were awed by
the simplicity and courage with which he read his Bible
and performed his devotions, as if alone, in the most
crowded hut. No one dared to make fun of him for being
so young and good.

About this time my father too went out to France,
with the Y.M.C.A., and was stationed at Rouen when
Edward went through on his way to the front lines.
They met and discussed whether Edward should return
to Aberdeen under the new regulation which released
medical students from military service in order to finish
their studies. In my father's attic room in a little French
hotel, they prayed together that he might still not be

required to fight. As a human being and a Christian the idea of destroying life was intolerable to him, as it was to my father.

When the German offensive opened in March my father was still in Rouen. He went daily to read the lists of the wounded and killed and missing pinned up at the British headquarters. My mother alone at Aberdeen—for Yda and I were on holiday in Glasgow with Aunt Helen—received a letter from grandfather in Birkenhead warning her that the casualties in France were so appalling, hardly anyone could escape unhurt. She wrote back rebuking him for his lack of faith, but dreamt vividly in the night of Edward, muddy and battle-stained, coming into her bedroom. He survived the offensive about a week, one night of which he spent building with his own hands a wooden bridge over a stream, in order that some of the guns might be withdrawn. On March 27th he was sent to hold a strategic point under heavy shell-fire. One of the mules in the gun-harness was wounded and Edward leapt off his horse to put the beast out of pain. As he shot it a piece of shrapnel struck him and severed the jugular vein. This was near Morcourt-sur-Somme.

As soon as she heard, my mother wrote to Aunt Helen and Uncle Norman asking them not to say anything to me and Yda but to arrange to send us home in two days, after a little family party to which she knew we were looking forward. A glance from Uncle Norman and a twittering gentleness in Aunt Helen may have put me on my guard. I read *Mr. Britling Sees it Through* as we travelled back to Aberdeen in the train, but only half knew what I read because of a strange mounting sense of tragedy. My mother was waiting for us on the platform and her face, so still and pale, spoke for her and spared our hearing what we already guessed. Her first words were simply that we must not weep and mourn, but be glad for him.

Letters soon came from my father. The day had arrived when Edward's name was added to the countless names upon the board. To me he quoted Bunyan, the last message of Mr. Valiant-for-Truth: 'My sword I give to him that shall succeed me in my pilgrimage, and my courage and skill to him that can get it.' Then there was Professor Cairns, confirming what my mother believed, saying that death must have been like the waking from a bad dream to a splendid summer morning: 'You remember the first summer morning of the holidays, the sheer delight of the weeks ahead crowding into the first hour.' So great was the fortitude of both my parents that we hardly plumbed beyond the surface of their profound grief at the time, but grew into the knowledge of it as the years passed—as the western world has slowly grown into the sense of what was squandered then, never to be replaced. The ranks of the survivors are searched and sifted for leaders, and the sword lies unclaimed.

It is all long ago, but memory challenges time and death. It moulds our sequent thoughts, turns the beam of all later knowledge into the further places of the beloved past, and teaches us to revise every judgment made in haste and ignorance. For those who remember, no account is ever closed and nothing in life however distant and deeply buried is quite lived out. Thirty years after, when the Second World War too was over, I picked up Sir Herbert Read's *In Retreat* in a casual, curious moment, and found that it was written about just those days in the end of March 1918, and of the battle line within a few miles of where Edward fought. I read with famished interest, filling up so many gaps in my knowledge and expecting as I turned each page to find the description of a fair young soldier who could be no one but Edward. But he was not there, and the little book left me conscious of a deeper silence still.